Praise for
What Would Grace Do?

One of VanityFair.com's
Summer 2013 Best Beach Reads

"*What Would Grace Do?* . . . help[s] you navigate life's dilemmas using lessons learned from the queen of elegance herself."
—*New York Post*

"For those wanting to live life like her highness, there's *What Would Grace Do?*, a guide . . . that covers everything from makeup to manners to flirting."
—*USA Today*

"Find out how fabulous life would be if all you did was in the style of Grace Kelly with *What Would Grace Do?*"
—*InStyle* (UK)

BILL COCKERILL

Gina McKinnon writes fiction, nonfiction, and humor. She lives in Brighton, England, with her husband and two children.

How to Live Life in Style
Like the Princess of Hollywood

What Would
Grace
Do?

Gina McKinnon

GOTHAM BOOKS

GOTHAM BOOKS
Published by the Penguin Group
Penguin Group (USA) LLC
375 Hudson Street
New York, New York 10014

USA | Canada | UK | Ireland | Australia | New Zealand | India | South Africa | China

penguin.com
A Penguin Random House Company

First published in Great Britain in 2012 by Aurum Press Ltd. under the same title

Previously published as a Gotham Books hardcover

First trade paperback printing, April 2014

10 9 8 7 6 5 4 3 2 1

Gotham Books and the skyscraper logo are trademarks of Penguin Group (USA) LLC

The Library of Congress has catalogued the hardcover edition as follows:

McKinnon, Gina.
What would Grace do? : how to live life in style like the princess of Hollywood /
Gina McKinnon.
p. cm.
"First published in Great Britain in 2012 by Aurum Press Ltd. under the same title."
Includes bibliographical references and index.
ISBN 978-1-592-40828-3 (hardcover)   ISBN 978-1-592-40875-7 (paperback)
1. Grace, Princess of Monaco, 1929–1982.   2. Women—Life-skills guides.
3. Women—Conduct of life.   I. Title.
HQ1221.M213 2013
646.7'0082—dc23   2012035124

Printed in the United States of America
Set in Berling Lt Std

For Lily-Belle,
the most elegant little lady I know.

~~~

Contents

Introduction   9

1. The Philadelphia Story   17

2. In the Movies   35

3. Love's Young Dream   61

4. The Grace Kelly Look   79

5. Ice-Cool Beauty   101

6. Royal Romance   119

7. Princess Grace   143

8. Family Ties   163

9. Friends for Life   179

10. Legacy   203

Acknowledgments   221

Bibliography   223

Index   229

Introduction

⌒⌒⌒

The Extraordinary Lives of Grace Patricia Kelly

FOR FIVE YEARS IN the 1950s, Grace Kelly was the Queen of Hollywood, but in 1956 she swapped her Tinseltown crown for a real one when exchanging "I do"s with Prince Rainier III of Monaco. Previously she had been a top model and a successful TV actress, and she would later become a doting mother and active philanthropist. Not to mention her position as a high priestess of style. In short, in her fifty-two years Grace Kelly lived many lives, and through them inspired generations of women. Certainly there are others—among them Jackie O, Audrey Hepburn, and Princess Diana—who have excited the fashion world, and yet still more who have lit up the silver screen or gripped a nation's hearts with their charitable deeds, but only Grace Kelly—model, actress, and princess—has done all three, and made it look effortless.

Made it *look* effortless. The truth is that Grace Patricia Kelly was a hard worker. From the age of seventeen when she attended the American Academy of Dramatic Arts in New York to her last moment on film (shot in 1982, the year she died), Grace strove for perfection in her work. Though her film career was rather short, with her well-chosen roles, some canny decision making, and of course her camera-friendly good looks, she shone on celluloid, becoming one of film's most adored and well-remembered actresses. Her faultless beauty and playful charm captured the hearts of the moviegoing public and a succession of male co-stars. And there aren't many Hollywood stars whose on-screen characters so closely resemble their real life, most significantly her turn as Princess Alexandra in *The Swan* (1956) preempting—as Hitchcock put it—her most enduring "last role" as wife to the Prince of Monaco.

Though her life as a princess was at times somewhat lonely, and her prince at times not so charming, she used her status as Her Serene Highness Princess Grace to change the lives of many and helped transform Monaco from a "sinking ship," as one wit put it, into a dream holiday destination for the rich and famous. It was in Monaco where Grace gave birth to her three children—the happiest and most treasured accomplishments of her life.

Before Rainier, Grace had experienced more than her fair share of the emotional turbulence of young love. She was "always falling in love" in her youth, she once said, and was rumored to have slept with many a male co-star . . . and a fair few others besides. Big, strong, older (and often married) men were her weakness. Some say this was because of the disappointment of her relationship with her domineering father, Jack Kelly. Others yet that she was a sexual predator, with a voracious appetite for passion. Such accusations only add to the mythology surrounding the (allegedly) promiscuous princess.

Of her legacy, though, perhaps the most enduring aspect is her innate sense of style; indeed sophistication and Grace Kelly go hand in white-gloved hand. She remains the unchallenged embodiment of refined glamour and poise, first appearing on America's Best-Dressed List in 1954 and setting a standard for elegance that has inspired women ever since, from *Mad Men*'s January Jones to Kate Middleton aka the Duchess of Cambridge. A whole look was named after her . . . and a scarf . . . *and* a handbag. You get the picture. Want an icon to reference for all things stylish? Look no further than Grace Patricia Kelly.

Like a cat with its nine lives, Grace reinvented herself time and again, adapting to whatever circumstance life threw at her, often acting on impulse and always, no matter what the task at hand, completing it with a perfection and professionalism that puts us lesser mortals to shame. Grace Kelly: model, actress, film star, princess, wife, mother, philanthropist, and campaigner . . . she did it all, and always with style and good grace.

HOW TO USE THIS BOOK

Phew, what a life! So rich with incident, accomplishment, and event—no wonder a whole queue of biographers were waiting in line to tell Grace Kelly's life story after the tragic accident that killed her in 1982. Some of those biographers have been kind, others . . . well, with a love life like our Gracie's (to use one of her nicknames) it is perhaps not surprising a few skeletons were dragged from closets.

But this is not another of those biographies. Yes, in the pages of this book you'll find biographical information—a veritable treasure trove of it, in fact, relating to the men, the movies, and *the* marriage, and much more besides. And for those of you who like the odd factoid, we share Grace's height, her favorite food, and all those other tidbits of information that make our heroine seem so much more *real*. But we only tell Grace's life story in relation to what you can learn from it. Because here's the rub: this little book is a "how to," a series of life lessons based on the triumphs and successes, as well as the mistakes, of an extraordinary woman. Here, we'll teach you how to handle everything from careers and cashmere to manners and men, from seduction and sex to bridesmaids and babies.

But these are not the ravings of a Kelly fanatic. Sure, we beat our drum for Grace Kelly and we beat it loudly, madly, enthusiastically. But just occasionally we lay our drumsticks to one side and allow a minute's quiet contemplation on her incongruities and failings, too. Both feted and reviled as an "Ice Queen," Grace Kelly was at times a divisive figure. While by all accounts warm, witty, and kind in her home life and with her co-stars, the media stirred up quite the different image of Grace as a pristine ice maiden, unapproachable and cold. We explore these diversities in this book, and study them to see what can be learned from them, also.

Not that we expect you to parrot Grace's lifestyle willy-nilly. Times have changed. Giving up a career for a man at the age of twenty-six would be unthinkable nowadays, and to wear a twin set, pearls, and gloves as you go about your daily business . . . well, it just seems *so* Miss Marple. And yet there are countless ways we can learn from la Kelly: how to make a go of your dreams, how to flirt, how to wear clothes well, how to negotiate the bumpy path of marriage. We could go on . . . and we will! And if you think doing what Grace

Kelly did is to disrespect the woman and her memory, remember the old saying: imitation is the sincerest form of flattery. And flatter Grace we do here, in spades.

So, now it's time to put your life on track and subpoena your inner Grace. As a witness in the vagaries of life, we can't think of anyone more expert than she.

chapter one

The Philadelphia Story

"If you're good enough, you're sure to reach the top."
KELLY FAMILY MOTTO

INTRODUCING GRACE KELLY: DAYDREAM BELIEVER

O N NOVEMBER 12, 1929, a future model and TV star, a future Queen of Hollywood, and a future Princess of Monaco—in short, a superstar—was born. But before all this, she was simply Grace Patricia, the third child of four of a wealthy Philadelphia family, born weeks before the stock market crash of 1929 when the Great Depression wreaked havoc across the United States. Appropriately enough, given the Kelly family business was in bricks and construction, Grace's father, Jack, was able to shelter his family from the worst of the storm, having kept his money in government bonds and cash, and so they continued to prosper during America's darkest economic days.

Grace and her siblings grew up in a spectacular seventeen-room mansion. It was a dream home with everything the children could wish for, including gorgeous rambling gardens to play in. A picture-book childhood—well, almost. It might be hard to imagine, but Grace always felt like the odd one out and the black sheep of her family. There was an older sister, Peggy, sporty and attractive (born four years before Grace); then older brother, John Junior (or "Kell"), a Jack Kelly miniature who would later become an Olympic oarsman like his father; and finally, the baby of the family, Lizanne, whose arrival brought out the green-eyed monster in the toddler-aged Grace. In comparison to these sportier, outdoor-loving siblings, Grace's character was distinctly different: she was far less robust, and prone to illness. It was as if she had been born with a cold, her family said.

Poor misunderstood Grace was introspective and thoughtful; a daydreamer in her own private world, who loved to read fairy tales and mythical stories, pen her own poems, and harbored an early ambition to be a ballet dancer. Jack Kelly wanted a team of track and field stars for children and was not taken with Grace's character, saving his approval for her stronger, sports-loving siblings. He just wasn't interested in artistic, intellectual Grace and her dreamy ways. Quite insensitively, he made no secret of the fact that he preferred Grace's more outgoing sisters and brother. But Jack Kelly was quite wrong to dismiss imaginative Grace's capacity to dream, for it was no idle waste of time.

In fact, Grace Kelly is a picture-perfect example of how, with ambition, hard work, and perseverance, a dreamer can make those dreams come true. And in what style! In later years, Jack would continue to profess his surprise when Grace became a household name.

"I thought it would be Peggy whose name would be up in lights one day," he said of Grace's elder sister to *McCall's* magazine in January 1955. Even when his daughter was clutching her Oscar he shook his head and wondered how quiet, sensitive Grace had been the one to achieve such glittering success.

Quite simply, Jack Kelly vastly underestimated the power of dreams and having the guts to strive to achieve them, even without the approval of those around you. Because, despite her lack of family support, Grace decided to follow her dream to become an artist and performer. In this chapter, we'll learn how she made it to the top in her chosen profession despite such familial disapproval and how you too can follow in Grace's elegantly faultless footsteps simply by using hard work, intelligence, and the subtle art of persuasion to achieve your own heart's desire. Jack Kelly may have coined the family motto, "If you're good enough, you're sure to reach the top," as an incentive for sporting prowess, but daughter Grace more than any of his offspring took those words to heart and turned her childhood dreams into reality.

DREAMTIME

But what's your dream? Before you can go out there and get it, you need to make time to figure out just what it is. Life can sometimes get so hectic it is easy to lose sight of what we truly want. So, what do you really want from your life? Are your dreams sparkling showstoppers like Grace's, or do you yearn for something a little more bijou, yet equally worthwhile?

Either way, it's time to do what your teachers always told you *not* to do, and get your head in the clouds and dream. Even if this doesn't seem your bag, and you're more of a feet-on-the-ground kind of girl, it might serve you well to float off a little and try one or all of the following:

○ MEDITATION. If meditation is your thing, it can be the perfect way to clear the mind and focus on you. If not, use your own tried-and-tested method to organize your thoughts. A warm bath or a long walk can work wonders, for example, to help you unwind and figure things out. (It's not a coincidence that Archimedes had his *Eureka!* moment in the tub.) Sometimes it's OK to be egocentric, so find a way to focus on your life and think about what you really want.

○ SLIP INTO THE SUBCONSCIOUS. If you're not the sort to daydream, perhaps listening to your subconscious at night might help. Why not keep a dream diary? This can be a very enlightening experience. Simply keep a journal by your bed and use it to jot down your dreams as soon as you wake. (Buy one with a lock if you want to keep out snoopers!) Or, if you prefer, there are many Web sites where you can keep online dream journals.

○ NEW BLANK DOCUMENT. Simply writing things down may give you the impetus to more energetically pursue your heart's desire: lists, dates in planners, random thoughts . . . they can all be useful. Why not write a New Year's ambition on the first day of each January? Seeing it written down there in black and white (or resolute red, if that's your thing) may just give you that extra edge to see your dreams fulfilled. And, if you want to find more ways of getting in touch with your subconscious, you could try taking a blank sheet of paper, or opening a blank document on your word processor and just start writing. See what appears. Once you have some idea what you're aiming for, get further inspired: take a bunch of magazines and make a collage, scrapbook, or mood board, about yourself and what you want to do with your life. Pinterest.com is a great way to organize your thoughts digitally, while drawing on inspiration from others who share your interests. But remember, simply putting a picture of Madonna in your scrapbook won't win you that Grammy just yet; you've got to work for it, too!

꩜ GET YOURSELF A PMA (Positive Mental Attitude). Don't underestimate the power of positive thinking. Once your idea is in place, settle back and spend some time imagining yourself living your dream: accepting that award, living in the perfect house, or holding that published novel in your hands.

꩜ GO BOOKISH. Still wondering what to do? There are lots of books out there designed to help you figure out your path. Get hold of a copy of *Your Best Year Yet!* by Jinny S. Ditzler or, if you're a creative type like Grace, try Julia Cameron's *The Artist's Way*.

All this planning, dreaming, and aspiring should make you feel all systems go, go, *go!* But if you're feeling more no, no, *no!* and panicking at how much you want to achieve, stop and smell the roses. Your dreams might seem lofty, but pause for a moment and write down a list of everything you have achieved in your life so far. You might just surprise yourself with the accomplishments you already have under your belt.

And remember, when you discover what you really want, don't let anyone discourage you. If you have a Jack Kelly in your life who just doesn't understand your dream, don't listen to their objections, go out there and prove your detractors wrong. It takes guts to follow your heart, especially when those you care about don't support you, but take heart from Grace's example: if you know, deep down inside, that a certain path is right for you, take it. Be bold and believe in yourself.

NEW YORK, NEW YORK

Of course our Grace knew just what she wanted. As a child she was already learning Shakespeare by heart and when she appeared in a school production of *Don't Feed the Animals* at the age of eleven, she even pulled a trick of pretending to drop her bag so she could whisper prompt lines to another young actress who had dried up on stage. Even grouchy Jack Kelly had to admit, "We've got a trouper on our hands."

So, aged just seventeen, plucky Grace decided to move to New York to study acting, despite her family being absolutely dead set against it. In fact, her father only agreed to her enrollment at the American Academy of Dramatic Arts because he thought that Grace would be home in a week. After all, it was only New York, not Hollywood she was going to.

But Grace would soon prove that assertion very wrong. And to calm those parental nerves about their darling daughter being adrift in the big, bad city, she agreed to live in the strictly buttoned-up Barbizon Hotel for Women. Over the years, the stately Barbizon has been home to such famous names as Lauren Bacall, Sylvia Plath, Candice Bergen, Ali MacGraw, and Liza Minnelli. Her parents' hope was that the hotel's strict rules—including the fact that no male guests were allowed past the ground floor—would protect young Grace (who had a notorious rebellious streak) from falling under the dissolute spell of New York City.

Even with the respectable Barbizon to call home, moving to the Big Apple must have seemed like a daunting move to Grace, but she knew that was where she needed to be to make it as an actress. To add to her stresses, initially she didn't get a place in the famous acting course at the illustrious American Academy of Dramatic Arts. But she didn't give up. Instead she asked to see the admissions board personally and used her persuasive charms to talk them into giving her a place.

Amazingly, it worked.

*T*ake a tip from Grace here. When you are following your dreams, don't give up as soon as you encounter that first hurdle. Fight for what you want and don't be afraid to take it to the top, where you can work your charms face-to-face. Remember, they can only say no, and who knows, they might just say yes.

AMERICA'S TOP MODEL

With her head down and acting studies her first priority, it came as something of a surprise when Grace's first taste of the entertainment industry, and life through a lens, came from a rather unexpected direction. In 1947, when she kindly agreed to accompany a friend from acting school to a modeling audition held by a top New

York agency, *she* was the one who was spotted. Grace's sweet gesture was well rewarded when she got the job instead.

The assignment was a huge success and, before long, she was signed up by the Walter Thornton Agency and offered a whole host of further modeling jobs. Her big blue-green eyes and even bigger smile photographed wonderfully and hers was the perfect look for 1950s Middle America. Grace's all-American girl-next-door looks were what the advertisers called nice clean stuff, and for them, she was a dream come true.

Grace was in high demand. With her perfect pout and flashing eyes, she hawked everything from Lux Soap with its famous "I'm a Lux Girl" slogan, to Old Gold cigarettes ("For a treat have a treatment—have an Old Gold!") to Lustre Cream shampoo ("Never dries, it beautifies!"). But she was never a high fashion model. Her classic looks were too mainstream for the runway. She did, however, appear on the covers of *Cosmopolitan* and *Redbook*. Not that she was in the business for the prestige of being a cover girl. Sure, the money was helpful, but the main thing Grace got from her time as a model was what she learned from the business of smiling for the camera.

Modeling also taught Grace how to stand. That effortless poise and posture, which became her elegant hallmark, was no doubt a legacy of modeling. In her later career Grace would know instinctively how to wear clothes, how to flatter her face and figure, and how to create a look.

It doesn't feel like a bad picture of Grace throughout her life, right up to her forties and fifties, was ever taken. She seems to instinctively know how to sit or stand to look her best—no doubt something she learned way back when. Grace also played with her own image in ways that were shocking at the time. One iconic image is a shot of her head rising out of a still pool of water. Taken by Howell Conant, the photo appeared on the cover of *Collier's* in June 1955. It was far from the controlled image the major studios liked to present of their actresses and Grace herself had had the idea. Before Grace, film stars simply weren't pictured with no makeup and wet hair, but this eye for the beauty of stark simplicity was to inspire a key part of her overall look for years to come and make her image so timeless.

In her modeling days, Grace might have been selling whichever product was signing her paycheck, but behind the scenes she was learning how to sell herself. Study any of her films, from *High Noon* to *High Society*, and it's crystal clear that Grace's iconic stature in the movies was helped no end by the fact she knew how to see herself from the outside—a legacy, no doubt, of all those hours posing for the tireless lens of the advertising industry's camera.

In one of Grace's most famous roles, Lisa Carol Fremont in Hitchcock's *Rear Window* (1954), she plays an ex-model. Costume designer and multi Oscar winner Edith Head was wowed. She said of Grace's innate sense of style: "She knew how to wear clothes . . . she was always very fastidious about the way she looked . . ." After working on *Rear Window*, Grace and Edith Head became lifelong friends and for years to come, she would be renowned as Head's favorite. And let's not forget Head was in huge demand with stars like Joan Crawford and Bette Davis, who were allegedly unwilling to don a single garment without her say-so.

All of this, you can do, too.

MODEL BEHAVIOR

OK, so we weren't all born with Grace's natural good looks. Even if we were, a catwalk career is beyond most people's reach, but there's no reason why you can't take a leaf out of Grace's book in learning to see yourself the way others see you and presenting yourself to the world like a top New York model. Here's how:

○ **MAKE FRIENDS WITH YOUR MIRROR.** To steal Grace's trick of knowing how to look your best, all you need is a full-length mirror and some good lighting. Natural light works best, so a big, bright window nearby, with lots of sunshine streaming through, is perfect. Otherwise, use plenty of lights and different lamps to avoid being stuck with one harsh overhead light source. As you might know from horrible experiences in chain store changing rooms, this is *never* flattering.

○ **STRIKE A POSE.** Flattering lighting solved, find a full-length mirror, stand in front of it in a variety of outfits, and pretend you're a Hollywood Queen floating down the red carpet. Have fun, but while you're at it, study yourself. Which is your best side? Time to find out. Perhaps like Grace you are lucky enough "not to have a bad side," as Cary Grant once said of the star (meaning her temperament as well as her classic good looks). Stand side-on, or check out your back view, peeking over one shoulder to recall that iconic image of Grace on the cover of this book. Compare side-on with your front view. Who designed your outfit? Now riffle through magazines featuring red-carpet pictures of your favorite stars, or do an image search online. Study how the most beautiful women in the world pose for the camera. Copy their poses and see which ones suit your face and figure.

⊙ BEST FACE FORWARD. Learn to present yourself perfectly and wherever you go, you will feel confident that you are showing your best face to the world. Moreover, you'll never again have to grimace at a bad holiday photo, or be forced to untag yourself on Facebook. Indeed, once you know how to pose like a pro, every photo of you will be picture perfect. And if they aren't, in these days of digital cameras, it's easy to hit delete.

⊙ SNAP HAPPY. And speaking of photographs, why not take the mirror project one step further? In the late 1940s Grace's modeling job meant that she got to see scads of pictures of herself. Use the opportunities afforded by digital cameras to take stacks of photos of yourself, too. Think advertising and sell yourself. Simply get to know how you look from the outside and how to show yourself off to your very best. Gain all the advantages Grace acquired from that modeling background—even if your looks are more conventional than catwalk.

STAND UP FOR YOURSELF

One of the greatest legacies of Grace's modeling career was her celebrated poise. Funnily enough, at 5'7" she felt too tall to be an actress and might easily have been more hunchback than heroine, had she given into the tall woman's curse: the slouch. Grace instinctively knew what standing poker-straight for shoots did for her. But you don't have to be a supermodel to be straight-backed and sensational: posture is all about developing the muscles you need to help you stand straighter, and with a little practice, you too can have Grace-like comportment. Here are some posture pointers:

YOGA. Exercise fads come and go but the ancient discipline of gentle movement into simple postures simply never goes out of style. Try an easygoing Iyengar class to improve your alignment with careful stretches, or look up the styles of yoga online to see what intensity suits you.

PILATES. Created by Joseph H. Pilates to build strength for his boxing, and once the beloved and closely guarded secret of ballerinas, this intense, targeted form of exercise has gone mainstream, thanks to Madonna et al. These magical exercises develop the core abdominal muscles and you may find if you do enough of them, you'll have a gorgeous 1950s corset-like posture *without* the agony of wearing one!

ALEXANDER TECHNIQUE. If you're really serious about perfecting your posture then you could try this technique (developed by an Australian actor in the 1890s), which now teaches good posture. The classes can be expensive so will only suit those willing to pay any price for the ultimate Grace-ification.

GAME CONSOLES. If you have a Wii console, why not try the Wii Fit, which uses a special device that you stand on to guide you through posture exercises? The Xbox Kinect has a similar program, too.

BALLET. It's not just for little girls in tutus as Natalie Portman shows (and then some) in *Black Swan*. Ballet has also been credited as the secret behind the exquisite looks of several silver-screen beauties, from Audrey Hepburn to Christina Hendricks. And Grace was a ballet belle, too. Lessons for adults are becoming more and more popular and the frills are optional (but oh, *so* much fun). More importantly, not only does ballet work every muscle but it's the easiest (OK, "easy" may be stretching things, and believe us, you'll be stretching!) route to perfect posture.

ACCENTUATE THE POSITIVE

No one can deny that Grace was a timeless beauty and today she is often touted as one of the most beautiful women who ever lived. In fact, you might well be thinking, It was all very well for *her*, looking like that—of course she charmed her way to the top.

Well, hold that thought. You might be surprised to know that in the beginning Grace was not the elegant beauty we know and love. Indeed, far from it. Believe it or not, when she first modeled TV commercials, her friends back home were completely surprised. Grace's showstopping good looks had never been obvious while she was growing up. It was only when she finally got in front of a camera that her glamour and charm were unmistakable.

But if cameras were to love Grace, while she posed and looked wonderful, there was still a problem when she opened her mouth to speak. Modeling success was all very well and good, but remember, Grace's dream was to act. And that meant speaking elegantly as well as looking good. Respiratory problems in childhood had left her with a flat, odd-sounding voice and the staff at the Academy thought it sounded too nasal and "misplaced." To counter this criticism, Grace took elocution lessons, which improved matters somewhat; they also had the effect of honing her Philadelphia twang into something more like a British accent—tones that suited her graceful upper-class look.

Later, when Grace was working in television, Margaret Kelly visited the set and would comment that her daughter's speech was affected. "Mother," said Grace, diligent as ever, "I'm working on it." Interestingly, when her movie career took off, Grace became well known for her trademark combo of that deep, upper-class twang coupled with her spectacular patrician beauty.

---

*S*o, if you find yourself fretting over your flaws (and we can't emphasize this too much), take heart from the fact that, as Grace's experience shows, nobody's perfect. Don't take it too hard if someone with your best interests at heart points out your imperfections; instead thank them for their honesty and take opportunities to improve yourself and learn. We're not saying that improving yourself is the same as aiming to be practically perfect in every way (only Mary Poppins managed that). Get better, but stay true to who you are and recognize your limitations. Perhaps that little flaw or quirk you can't overcome will even become your own, much-admired, much-envied hallmark.

But the main thing to learn from Grace's modeling work is to make the most of opportunities. Follow your goal, but pay close attention to the opportunities you might never have thought of. Remember John Lennon's famous quote, "Life is what happens to you while you're busy making other plans." Something might come along that may not be exactly what you want, but pause before you dismiss it out of hand. Make sure you don't miss out on any chances to learn new skills that could help pave the path to your dreams.

At this point, it's also worth noting some wise words from supermodel Helena Christensen: "When you are modeling," she said, "you are creating a picture, a still life, perhaps something like a silent film. You convey emotion but you are only using your body." There's no doubting that Grace picked up a few ideas about expression and comportment from her days as a model in the late forties, too.

THE LITTLE BREAKS

Grace's talent and hard work finally paid off when, not long after graduation from the Academy, she was spotted by a producer from a Pennsylvania theater and offered a place in their repertory company. Coincidentally her first major role was in a play written by her uncle (George Kelly), *The Torch Bearers*, at The Bucks County Playhouse in 1949. But there was no nepotism at hand here. "If I don't do it by myself, I don't want to do it," was a mantra running through Grace's life.

In 1949, after rep, Grace auditioned for a part in a revival of *The Father* by intense Swedish playwright August Strindberg, and despite her modest experience she won the role. (It is interesting to note her character struggles for independence from her close-knit and loving, but misunderstanding parents.) Grace later explained that she felt she was lucky to land the part because she had so often been told that she was too tall for the roles she wanted. She only got the part, she felt, because the actors cast as her parents were also relatively tall. Interestingly, even as she was crowned Hollywood's Queen, she never scored another Broadway role. Maybe that towering height was more of a hindrance, after all.

---

*W*hatever the truth behind Grace's casting in *The Father*, she seized the opportunity in both hands and spent her free time from performing in the play with the other, more experienced actors in the cast, sitting in their dressing rooms chatting and soaking up all the advice they had to give her about a career in show business. This high-profile role led to work in the burgeoning television industry and hardworking Grace appeared in more than fifty live television shows, most notably in *Rich Boy* (1952), a drama based on F. Scott Fitzgerald's short story of the same name. At one point her hectic schedule made her one of the busiest TV actresses in the business. According to then producer Delbert Mann: "She very quickly became a member of the stock company: those actors that we could cast over and over again."

These days we're used to stories of sudden celebrity. Really, anyone can be famous for fifteen minutes, and after only about fifteen minutes' effort. It's as if we hope for some instant formula that will magic our names up in lights. Sure, with Grace alchemy was at play to some degree, but it wasn't just her natural on-screen chemistry with her co-stars that saw her reach supernova levels of fame: all those TV dramas, the repertory theater, her Academy training, the ballet, the elocution lessons, and sheer hard work made up her down-to-earth formula for success.

So, by the time her breakthrough role did appear, Grace had spent hours and hours refining her craft. Want fame in an instant? Forget it, and don't be afraid to make like Grace and take the slow boat to your dream destination. Remember, the journey is important too, and sometimes it's better to take your time, enjoy the view, and chat to your fellow passengers, and before you know it, you will have *arrived*!

The Astonishingly Beautiful Grace Kelly's Formula for Success:

Hard work + Perfectionism + Beauty^3 = SUCCESS

chapter two

In the Movies

"Miss Grace P. Kelly—a famous star of stage and screen."
PROPHECY FROM GRACE'S HIGH SCHOOL YEARBOOK, 1947

HOORAY FOR HOLLYWOOD!

MODEL, SOCIALITE, PRINCESS, GRACE Kelly was—and through
her movies channeled—all these roles. Though her film career was
rather short (she all but retired at just twenty-six after making
eleven movies), Grace worked tirelessly for the right roles and decisions. Along with her camera more-than-friendly good looks, she
remains one of film's most beloved and remembered stars. In 1956
she was voted the Golden Globe's World Film Favorite Actor,
Female, and in 1999 she was ranked thirteenth top female actor ever
by the American Film Institute.

There can't be many Hollywood stars whose on-screen personas
so closely resemble their real life. In Grace's case her dazzling turn
as Jimmy Stewart's girlfriend, Lisa Fremont, in Hitchcock's *Rear
Window*, recalled her earlier modeling career; as socialite Tracy Lord

in *High Society*, her wealthy Philadelphia upbringing comes to mind; and her top billing as Princess Alexandra in *The Swan* preempted her "last role" (as Hitchcock called it) as a real-life princess.

Grace came to the movies after Hollywood's golden age, but a nasty hangover from those times remained, the bête noir of 1950s movie stars: the studio system. Under this system stars would sign away their lives to the big studios for that much-sought-after contract, which nevertheless shackled them in "golden handcuffs" and often contained bizarre contractual obligations. (Joan Crawford's contract, for instance, stipulated what time she should go to bed.) Always the studios themselves and not the creatives were in a movie's driving seat.

Well, Grace was not inclined to be a passenger. Following the advice of her playwright uncle George, she refused to sign a Hollywood contract not once but twice (in the late 1940s and early 1950s). But in 1952 along came a temptation too great even for our levelheaded, career-minded rising star: a starring role alongside Clark Gable. Filmed on location in Africa? Yes, *please!* Yielding to temptation, Grace signed a six-year contract to make three movies a year with MGM, but only on the understanding that she could still live in New York and take time out to do theater. According to legend, this contract was signed at the airport check-in desk prior to flying out for filming. For the first (but by no means last) time in her life a snap decision and following her intuition would stand Grace in good stead.

Clever girl!

But it wasn't just intuition that brought her success; Grace achieved all this and more via her tenacity, her quiet resolution, her dedication, and sheer hard work—all things we'll cover in this chapter.

We'll then go on to uncover what you too can learn from her movie-star success. Not that we claim to have the secret recipe for stardom on celluloid, but what we do possess are a few key ingredients to help you achieve whatever you set your sights on, even if your life's ambition is one more akin to good home cooking than haute cuisine.

Time, then, to find a comfy chair and your specs, break out the popcorn, and dim the lights as we head to the movies.

High Noon

Remember Grace's hard work during her stint as a TV actress? Well, it finally paid off when she bagged a small role as Mrs. Louise Ann Fuller in the movie *14 Hours* (1951). The suspense drama wasn't a great success but it led to Gary Cooper, no less, spotting Grace and asking for her to be cast as his Quaker wife in his new movie, *High Noon* (1952). Of Grace, Cooper said: "I thought she looked pretty and different and that maybe she'd be somebody. She looked educated and as if she came from a nice family. She was certainly a refreshing change from all these sexballs we've been seeing so much of."

With its almost real-time plotting scored by the lilting strains of "Do not forsake me, oh my darlin' . . . ," *High Noon* would end up being one of the most famous Westerns of all time. It's easy to see why a movie such as this would appeal to the kindhearted, morally courageous Grace. The film relentlessly focuses on the theme of taking a stand and doing what you know is right, even when no one else supports your actions. (Jack Kelly and his lack of support for Grace's acting career, anyone?) Marshal Will Kane (Gary Cooper) defends his town from the revenge-seeking Miller gang. Despite the song, Kane *is* forsaken: he is deserted by everyone in town until eventually his young pacifist wife comes to his aid.

The film was a real crowd pleaser for its 1951 audience and, with its clever plotting, snappy dialogue, and palpable tension, more than stands up to the scrutiny of the sophisticated modern film viewer. However, at the time Grace's pivotal role was somewhat overlooked. Also, she was miscast: at twenty-one playing the wife of a character in his fifties. Not that such miscasting doesn't take place today. Think Angelina Jolie cast as Colin Farrell's mother in the 2004 movie *Alexander* (she was just one year older than Farrell). *Plus ça change, plus c'est la même chose,* as the French say, particularly in Hollywood.

Overall, *High Noon* was no career high for Grace. The experienced actress Katy Jurado sizzles on screen while Grace is wan and somewhat tentative. With our Grace fan hats on we might make excuses and say her character is scripted that way, but in truth, it's not her best effort. Grace herself was not a fan of the film, thinking she hadn't known enough about screen acting to do it justice. A director friend of her's, Ted Post, recalls that Grace felt her eyes were "flat" and that she wanted them to "shine with meaning."

Though an iconic and fitting start for Grace, *High Noon* had not been the long-awaited Big Break. Which is why, when the desert dust had settled, twenty-one-year-old Grace saddled up her metaphorical horse and rode on back to New York to hone her craft under the guidance of acting guru Sanford (Sandy) Meisner, her spot in the limelight still a speck on the Western horizon.

High Noon—The Yee-Hahs

Grace's first high-profile film role in a movie showered with awards.

High Noon—The Neighs/Nays

Grace's role was underwritten and she was possibly miscast, leaving her in the shadow of her more experienced, much older co-star, as well as the popular actress from Mexican cinema, Katy Jurado.

A LIFE LESSON FROM GRACE

Take a tip from Grace here by not getting downhearted and learning to shrug off disappointments. If something seems like your Big Break into your dream career and then it doesn't pan out that way, do your best to simply shake it off and get on with the next task at hand. Think of Grace after *High Noon* and remember that if you work hard and have talent, opportunity might just knock twice.

Mogambo

And Hollywood did come knocking on Grace's door again with African epic *Mogambo* (1953). Adventure stories in exotic locations had taken off with the advent of color films, perhaps partly because foreign travel was still way beyond the budget of most people. Thanks to the magic of the movies, it became possible to see the world.

By the time MGM decided they wanted Grace for a role in their latest exotic epic, she was happy with her life in New York. In fact, she almost turned down the part. It might sound like a dream come true: a role in a big movie from a top studio, opposite Clark Gable—King of Hollywood himself—but Grace was no pushover, not even for the willful head (Dore Schary) of studio giant Metro-Goldwyn-Mayer. And here we have a perfect example of the art of steely compromise. More than that, Grace knew her worth and even when her dreams came calling, she remained cool, she was clear about what she wanted . . . and she held out until she got exactly that.

Later, Grace even admitted that she only took the role because she wanted to visit Africa; even brushing up on the local dialect (Swahili) before jetting off, so keen was she on the trip. And let's not forget she was attracted by the wildlife and scenery (and we don't just mean the lions and tigers): we mean *you*, Mr. Gable!

Mogambo—The Wildest Dreams

For Grace, that trip to Africa. More generally, another chunky role in a high-profile picture, with another famous co-star: this time, Clark Gable. And professionally, she was beating a path to the movie star Hall of Fame: winning a Golden Globe for Best Supporting Actress (1954), and being nominated for an Oscar for Best Actress in a Supporting Role.

Mogambo—The Bump Back Down to Earth

Sadly, the role as a two-dimensional wife of an academic was underwritten, and Grace had to suffer another director (John Ford), who was less than supportive. "I really wasn't very good in *Mogambo*," she said later, a nagging self-doubt about her performance that would characterize her entire career. And of all her movies this one doesn't stand the test of time too well, either.

A LIFE LESSON FROM GRACE

Know your own worth and hold out for what you truly want. If an amazing opportunity lands at your feet, don't lose your self-respect. Think hard about what you really want and what's most important to you. After all, maybe, just maybe, that dream job needs you more than you need it. And don't let others underestimate you. Studio head Dore Schary, taking Grace for this year's ditzy blonde, deserved this pithy retort in an interview in *Time* magazine from our heroine: "If anybody starts using me as scenery, I'll do something about it."

Dial M for Murder

So once again with *Mogambo*, Grace had ended up disappointed in a performance that left her feeling less than an African queen. At this point in the story, the key to unlocking her spellbinding screen presence was still to be found.

Enter, stage left, one of the most popular and successful film directors of all time. Why, hello there, Mr. Alfred Hitchcock!

Strangely, Hitchcock saw the same rejected screen test (for the movie *Taxi* in 1952) that John Ford had seen before deciding to cast Grace in *Mogambo*. Just how important did that one screen test turn out to be? And it's even more surprising when you consider that Grace didn't get the part for which she was actually auditioning at the time the screen test was made. Talk about snatching success from the jaws of failure . . . twice over!

Hitchcock was a smart cookie. Right away, he saw Grace's potential and snagged her (loaning her to Warner Bros. from MGM on the cheap) for a pivotal leading role as Margot Mary Wendice in his adaptation of the stage hit of the suspenseful murder mystery, *Dial M for Murder* (1954). Filming began and Grace was happier on this particular set than she had ever been. She was so confident that when she had to appear in her bedclothes in the pivotal attempted murder scene, she suggested she might wear a sheer nightgown instead of a less-revealing velvet dressing gown, reasoning a woman alone in her apartment wouldn't get all bundled up in a robe if she was woken up in the middle of the night to answer the phone.

Hitchcock took her advice and if you check out the scene in question, you'll see the result was pretty stunning. Grace looks gorgeous, but also when the chilling attack takes place it is all the more horrifying because in her nightgown, she is so fragile and vulnerable.

Buoyed by the confidence gained from this suggestion Grace went on to make changes to her makeup design when her character was in prison, arguing against the heavy rouge suggested. She reasoned, again very logically, that full makeup simply wouldn't be feasible in that situation. Good call, Grace.

Dial M for Murder—The Ring-a-Ding-Dings!

Finally, a director who really got what made Grace special and valued her unique qualities. He may have been another tyrant on the set, but Hitchcock was very impressed with her work on the movie. No wonder Grace was his number-one choice as leading lady from that point on.

Dial M for Murder—The "Wrong Number"

Despite his enthusiasm, Grace wasn't sure what Hitchcock thought of her performance. The public loved it, though. Not to mention the critics, who selected Grace as Best Actress in 1954, with newspaperman Hartford Courant reporting: "Grace Kelly Tops Poll of Critics in New York," based on her work in the picture (and others filmed in 1954).

A LIFE LESSON FROM GRACE

Speak up and offer your ideas. Even if you are talking to masters of their craft, you might have a fresh take or an original idea. The best people will always listen to suggestions, no matter how successful or talented they might be.

Rear Window

Around the time of filming *Rear Window*, Grace met one of her great loves, Oleg Cassini. These days, fashion designer Cassini is best known for his creation of Jackie Kennedy's trademark look. But before the First Lady, he cut his teeth on another future style icon. Back then, he was Grace's first big romance and was to become her fiancé.

Naturally, our Grace did not let romance distract her from the dogged pursuit of her career goals. In fact, when she was offered a role in *On the Waterfront* (1954), which meant she could stay with Cassini in New York as the gritty movie was to be filmed there, she said no. Because there was another offer on the table: another offer from movie maestro Alfred Hitchcock. Given only one hour by her agent Jay Kanter to decide which movie to go for, Grace decided to go with her gut. It proved to be a smooth move. At last, as she desired, her eyes "shine with meaning," her expressions are entrancing and intriguing, her dialogue sprightly, clever, and quick. We may have our Grace-tinted glasses on here, but we have to say this is one of the best performances ever in a Hitchcock movie.

What Hitchcock loved about Grace was that ice maiden, "look, but don't touch" on-screen persona, what he called her "sexual elegance" and what he wanted for *Rear Window*. The command for this wish to appear in the movie was given to Edith Head, Hitchcock's costume designer, whom he instructed to design a variety of floaty, virginal-looking gowns that Head herself described thus: "Hitch wanted her [Grace] to appear like a piece of Dresden china, something slightly untouchable."

It would be fair to say that in *Rear Window*, Edith Head's magic worked wonders as Grace drifts across the screen in those flowing gowns, lush and ethereal all at once.

Rear Window—
The (Rear) Window of Opportunity

At last came Grace's real breakthrough. Her performance was praised to the skies by the critics and allowed her to display both her intelligence and quiet sensuality. According to co-star Jimmy Stewart, Grace seemed to know the movements before Hitchcock did. In the crucial scene where Lisa Fremont climbs the ladder to peek into the suspected murderer's apartment block, Grace acted on intuition and Hitchcock went with her take on the scene.

*Rear Window—*Simply Window Dressing?

But some critics said that playing an ex-model and society queen wasn't much of a stretch for Grace. Could she perhaps be in danger of becoming typecast?

A LIFE LESSON FROM GRACE

The fact that Hitchcock rated Grace so highly over other, more obvious sex goddesses just goes to show that, tempting as it may be, comparing yourself to others is a nonstarter. There may be people around you who seem to have more obvious charms or who are achieving roaring successes and getting right where you want to be, but remember, the race is long. Sometimes you're in front and sometimes you're behind, but the only achievements that really matter are yours.

And if your next-door neighbor lands that dream job, bags that dreamboat hunk, or fulfills your wildest dreams, play nice! Grace was, well, gracious in both her work and everyday life and would certainly not have succumbed to the green-eyed monster.

Oh, and don't forget her cool reasoning at the choice between *On the Waterfront* and *Rear Window*—and all in under sixty minutes. We probably need hardly mention this, but compromising your dreams for the sake of romance is not the Grace Kelly way. Well, not unless you're offered something truly beyond your wildest dreams, but we'll get to that. . . .

The Country Girl

After *Rear Window* Grace's career was flying and she was in high demand, but to her dismay she was mainly typecast as the upper-class ice queen. And, as we know well, she could play this in her sleep. Not that interesting roles for a beautiful twenty-something actor were flying out the studios. As Mark Cousins writes in his *Story of Film*, in 1950s cinema: "Many US filmmakers were happy with the conventional, consumerist, optimistic picture of American life in the Eisenhower years."

Luckily for Grace, directors such as George Seaton wanted to buck the trend and adapted a play called *The Country Girl* into a downbeat drama for the big screen, which tells of an alcoholic actor and his attempts to revive his career. Now, our Grace was a skilled actress who had spent hours and hours training and honing her craft. She was determined to prove it and that's why she went all out to get the role of Georgie Elgin, the actor's wife.

This hard-hitting movie would prove a massive stretch for Grace, moving away from her roles playing classy well-dressed socialites and channeling a dowdy, put-upon, drably clad wife. But MGM preferred to play it safe: they wanted Grace to carry on as the classy bit of window dressing. As always, Grace aimed high and held out for more; she even threatened to retire from the movies altogether if she didn't get the part she wanted. The picture's producer William Perlberg told *Time* magazine in 1955 that Grace had said to MGM: "If I can't do this picture, I'll get on the train and I'll never come back. I'll quit the picture business. I'll never make another film."

When, thanks to her tenacity, she was cast in the movie, the film's lead (Bing Crosby) was dead against Grace taking the role. He pronounced her too pretty (and he would know), but as *we* know, Grace was so much more than a talking clotheshorse, and now here was her chance to show it. And before long, Crosby, like many of Grace's detractors before him, was singing a different tune. Though he had endless objections to her playing the part, he soon ate his words when filming began and would simply say, "She's great!"

It's a tense and dramatic movie as downtrodden Georgie falls for the producer (William Holden) of her husband's comeback play. A key moment of Grace's successful portrayal is when said producer realizes he is attracted to Georgie and she murmurs, "Nobody has looked at me as a woman for years." Here is Grace, one of the world's most beautiful women, but at that moment we believe 100 percent in those words. Makeup free and in shabby clothes a million sartorial miles from her usual designer wardrobe, the world woke up to the relentless talent of one very special star. In fact, she was nominated for an Oscar and, much to the chagrin of Judy Garland, the favorite, went on to win! "You took what was rightfully mine," Garland is alleged to have balled down the phone to Grace in a heated post-Oscar-night conversation.

In itself, Grace's Oscar speech was a thing of beauty. Almost unrecognizable these days when it's almost obligatory for every Oscar acceptance to be accompanied by a histrionic nervous breakdown, she seems languidly understated. Dressed in a breathtakingly simple silvery blue gown designed by one of her favorites, Helen Rose, she held her statuette and said, "The thrill of this moment keeps me from saying what I really feel. I can only say thank you with all my heart to all who made this possible for me."

The Country Girl—The Green Pastures

Ding *dong*! Hello? *Oscar!*

What's more, here was a director in George Seaton who appreciated all those hours Grace had spent honing her craft. In 1955, he waxed lyrical: "Grace doesn't throw everything at you in the first five seconds. Some girls give you everything at once and there it is, there's no more. But Grace is like a kaleidoscope: one twist and you get a whole new facet."

The Country Girl—The Dung Heaps

OK, there were the dowdy outfits, the bare-faced look (makeup free), not to mention the grim subject matter. But, well, easily outweighed by the pros on this one.

A LIFE LESSON FROM GRACE

Take a long look at that (short) Oscar speech and understand when less is more. Sometimes a simple gesture can make the most impact. A brief but heartfelt thanks, in person or via a note, can mean so much more than a gushing, self-involved performance that is more about you than those you claim to be thanking.

*I*n 1954, sandwiched on either side of filming *The Country Girl*, Grace made two movies under contract to MGM, neither of which can be said to be her best work. As the company still floundered over which roles to give her, she was loaned to Paramount to make the war film *The Bridges at Toko-Ri* (1954), playing the wife of a naval pilot who fears she may be left a widow. A high-octane movie "flawed by mawkish sentimentality," according to the *Time Out* film guide, this is one case where being famous for only fifteen minutes proves a blessing: Grace is only onscreen for that amount of time. Later that year after filming *The Country Girl*, she traveled to South America to star as a coffee plantation owner alongside Stewart Granger's emerald hunter to make the now widely acknowledged dud, *Green Fire* (1954). She wasn't keen to make the picture but it was the only way MGM would loan her to Paramount so that she could take that sought-after role of Georgie. Even MGM Head Dore Schary would later say of *Green Fire*: "It was a dog."

There are two important life lessons from Grace here. Number one: fulfill your obligations. In no line of work do you want to get a reputation for being a contract breaker. Dutiful Grace had learned in childhood to respect her elders and supposed betters, and played this part to a T here. Number two lesson is the art of compromise: by conceding to MGM to make *Green Fire*, Grace got her dream ticket to film *The Country Girl*, even if the journey via South America was a bit of a bumpy (and long) ride! So, if compromise makes you break out in a stubborn sweat, just let those pearls of perspiration drip off you: who knows what a little give-and-take might bring?

To Catch a Thief

After making two movies together, and with such awesome results, it came as no surprise when Hitchcock wanted Grace for another starring role. In fact, he is often quoted as saying he bought the script for *To Catch a Thief* (1955) with Grace in mind as his leading lady. The picture is a sparkling, thrilling comedy set in the South of France, a part of the world obviously to become very significant to Grace, for it was while filming there that she caught her first-ever glimpse of Monaco.

Grace plays Frances (Francie) Stevens, a daring woman out for thrills, who becomes entangled in the paws of a seductive cat burglar (Cary Grant). It's a sophisticated, gorgeous-looking film, Grace's natural home. And now that she had *The Country Girl* under her belt she could relax and enjoy the frivolity of this sun-kissed flick. Grace loved working with Cary Grant as they shared a sense of humor, a characteristic brought to the fore when Hitchcock asked them to improvise some dialogue and they dared each other to get as risqué as they could. Here's the best bit from that classic roadside innuendo-laden picnic scene:

> FRANCIE: I've never caught a jewel thief before. It's so stimulating! [She offers him a piece of cold chicken.]
> Do you want a leg or a breast?
> ROBIE: You make the choice.
> FRANCIE: Tell me, how long has it been?
> ROBIE: Since what?
> FRANCIE: Since you were in America last?

It's no surprise that Grant, who had appeared alongside some of the greatest names in Hollywood, such as Marlene Dietrich, Katharine Hepburn, and Marilyn Monroe, fell for Grace and the pair became lifelong friends. He said of her: "She was the most beautiful woman I'd ever known. She had the most incredible ESP about me. She could almost read my thoughts. She was cool and reserved and then she'd say something about my own mood or attitude and it was like she was completely tuned in."

To Catch a Thief—The Peaks

Oh, the fun, the glamour! Not to mention that all-important first glimpse of Monaco and its rolling hills.

To Catch a Thief–The Troughs

Some might say that this particular movie marked the beginning of the end. It was to be Grace's last film with her beloved Hitchcock at the helm.

A LIFE LESSON FROM GRACE

Never be afraid to have fun. You might be hitting the heights in your dream career, you might even have your job's equivalent of an Oscar (round of applause!), but don't think that means you have to come over all earnest *Country Girl* Grace. Imitate her pleasure in filming *To Catch a Thief*: put on your metaphorical sunglasses, put down the roof on an open-top car, hook up with a cat burglar (optional), and throw caution to the wind. In other words, find ways to have fun, relax, and enjoy your success. After all, if you can't do that, what's the point?

High Society

Grace's last two movies were the height of sophistication. *The Swan*, a tale of a princess, was followed up with the musical romance, *High Society* (both 1956). Appropriately enough, given Grace's background, this was a musical adaptation of the classic 1940s romantic comedy, *The Philadelphia Story*. As with *Dial M for Murder*, Grace, as a stage actress at heart, was always drawn to movie roles that had their roots in the theater. And here, waiting in the wings, was a film that could almost have been written for her. In fact, when Tracy Lord's mother (played exquisitely by Margalo Gillmore) describes her as "exceptionally strong-minded and very wonderful, always," she could almost certainly be describing Grace.

As a musical *High Society* hits all the right notes, featuring both Bing Crosby as Grace's ex-husband and Frank Sinatra as a newspaper reporter, with whom she almost has a fling. The musical numbers mostly featured these two tuneful heavyweights, along with musical star Celeste Holm and jazz legend Louis Armstrong, who appeared in a cameo role. And among these musical heavy-hitters, Grace herself was required to sing one of the numbers: "True Love," a charming duet with Crosby. Imagine how daunting that must have been to Grace, who didn't consider herself a singer and had never sung in public. But performing that song was a key part of a role she wanted madly, so she went for it. The Cole Porter number turned out to be a hit. When released as a single, Grace ended up with a gold record to take its place next to her cherished Oscar—much to the chagrin of Frank Sinatra, who never received the same accolade. Much later in the 1960s Prince Rainier, tired of hearing Sinatra bemoan this fact, had a gold record made for Ol' Blue Eyes to put a stop to his green-eyed goings-on!

High Society—The High Notes

So, a gold record for a duet with Bing Crosby, no less, but more importantly, Grace shows her range as an actor, displaying a distinct flair for musical comedy. She plays on her reputation as a spoiled Philadelphia socialite, so when she pirouettes in to fool roving reporter Frank Sinatra, the audience relishes her self-mockery and the comedy works on two levels.

High Society—The Bum Notes

This was to be Grace's last film, and one that her future husband Prince Rainier rather wished had ended up on the cutting-room floor.

A LIFE LESSON FROM GRACE

Try something new every once in a while. You never know, you might like it! And who knows what hidden talents you might discover.

Roll Credits

High Society turned out to be Grace's last movie and she never did complete the six-year contract for MGM that she wrangled over all those years before. But the end of her film career was not so clear-cut as a dream wedding and a husband who wanted to keep her all to himself. In fact, years after her famous marriage to a prince, she considered going back to Hollywood for her beloved Alfred Hitchcock to star in *Marnie* (1964).

The truth is that although Grace had enjoyed a glowing career she grew tired of Hollywood. All the way she'd had to fight for parts that were appropriate and, Hitchcock aside, even when she landed plum roles she found herself cast against much older actors, performing supporting roles that were underwritten and so she ended up being overlooked. What's more, as her movie career accelerated, she missed her beloved theater. Later she would tell her biographer Donald Spoto, "I never really liked Hollywood. I found it unreal—unreal and full of men and women whose lives were confused and full of pain. To outsiders it looked like a glamorous life, but it really was not."

So, to finish, here's another point to pick up on: it may seem crazy, right at the start, but do consider the fact that you might achieve your dream (and more) but still end up feeling unfulfilled. Grace had her dreams all sewn up by the tender age of twenty-six but was beginning to wonder whether her dream was all it was cracked up to be. What's more, she never did shake those feelings of self-doubt. "I don't think I was accomplished enough as an actor to be remembered as that particularly," she would say in the last interview before her death in 1982, going on with characteristic humility: "I don't feel I achieved much more in my movie career to stand out from other people."

But the end of her movie career was not the end of Grace's time in the spotlight. Au contraire. Something else was on the horizon and she had already set her heart on a brand-new dream.

MOVIE-STAR MANNERS

"Grace Kelly was the least prima-donna-like actress I ever knew."

JOHN ERICSON, GRACE KELLY'S *GREEN FIRE* CO-STAR

Before we leave this chapter and move on to Grace's men (settle down there at the back!), it's important to highlight one more aspect of Grace's star quality: her impeccable manners, thoughtfulness, and down-to-earth behavior. Whether you sweep streets, head up a bank, or sing for your supper, these attributes are must-haves for your own social repertoire and work ethic.

Don't forget this was at a time when directors had to deal with all manner of hotheadedness from their stars. While troubled Marilyn had them tearing their hair out with her tawdry tantrums, and while Judy Garland and Ava Gardner found inspiration from the bottom of a bottle, Grace had her mentors and co-stars swooning over her impeccable good manners. Although she appeared in just eleven films over five years, she made a dramatic impact on the film world; her steadfast belief in herself changing the way actors in the movies were treated forever. Grace fought for the parts she wanted and used the press and her own image in canny ways to get what she desired and prove her talent.

Unheard of!

With these things in mind, let's take a few minutes to learn a few lessons as to how Grace dealt with a trio of the trickier aspects of stardom: the press, her fans, and her co-stars.

SO, HOW DID GRACE ...

DEAL WITH THE PRESS? As we've seen, Grace was something of a mold-breaker in her flat refusal to take the roles offered her by the studio. Before her, most actors had simply done as they were told. Annoyed by her refusals, MGM sidelined her—not offering her starring movie roles at all, something that could do big damage to her career. Normally being sidelined by a studio like this was seen as an embarrassment for the actor involved and they kept quiet, but Grace went straight to the press and told them of her shoddy treatment. She was their darling from that point on, even if her opinion of them was less than flattering: "The freedom of the press works in such a way that there is not much freedom from it," she once famously said.

Grace's handling of the press would also come in handy later while traveling by ship to Monaco in 1956 for her wedding when besieged by a brigade of peeping paparazzi. Instead of camping out all day in her cabin (as she yearned to do), she organized a daily press conference to send updates to both sides of the Atlantic, which kept the yapping paps at her heels . . . well, mostly.

And here then is another top tip that we can take from Grace's experience: if someone is hounding you, be it a boyfriend, girlfriend, colleague, or family member, throw them the occasional bone because a little attention goes a long way toward keeping the dogs at bay.

. . . **RELATE TO HER FANS?** Whether celebrity, layperson, or royalty (Hollywood or actual), Grace had a manner with others befitting of her name—and that included her fans. In fact, her former PA Louisette Levy-Soussan Azzoaglio recalls how far bighearted Grace would go to please them: "Each year, this woman would arrive at the palace with scrapbooks of cuttings, all of them featuring Princess Grace. Instead of recoiling in horror, or sending a minion to deal with her, Grace would insist on meeting the woman herself, and having tea with her. Every year they would mull over her articles and enjoy a chat. Over the years, the two women became friends. They never missed their annual meeting."

The life lesson here is a no-brainer: what goes around comes around, kid! In as much as you may want to unleash your inner diva, it's probably best to keep the feather boa in the wardrobe if you want a piece of lady luck.

. . . GET ALONG WITH HER CO-STARS AND OTHERS ON SET? Well, what do *you* think? "Every man who was ever lucky enough to work with Grace Kelly fell in love with her," Herbert Coleman, assistant director of *Rear Window*, once stated, while both Jimmy Stewart and Cary Grant named her their favorite co-star. And as for being Alfred Hitchcock's muse, well, we'll get to that . . .

In the meantime, here's another Grace-inspired formula for all you Kelly copycats:

Good Breeding + Talent + Warmth, Wit, and Charm = Everyone's Favorite Leading Lady

VITAL STATISTICS

Grace in Numbers

Number of TV appearances: 40 plus

Grace earned $120 a week for her first movie role
in *14 Hours*

Grace made eleven movies in just five years

Zero stand-ins were used for Grace's horse riding in
High Noon and fencing in *The Swan*

She could only see about six feet in front of her
due to acute myopia. Grace loved the chance to wear
her glasses in the movie *The Country Girl*

100 yards of silk were used to make her
Helen Rose wedding gown

She has a star on the Walk of Fame at
6329 Hollywood Blvd.

Grace was ranked 51 in *Empire* (UK) magazine's
"The Top 100 Movie Stars of All Time" list

She was named #13 Actress on the American Film
Institute's 50 Greatest Screen Legends

chapter three

Love's Young Dream

"When I was younger I was always falling in love."

GRACE PATRICIA KELLY

A PLETHORA OF PARAMOURS, SOME teenage kicks, and a fairy-tale romance, not to mention the fictional fellas—the love life of Grace Patricia Kelly has more than enough characters to form the script of a Hollywood bonkbuster, if you believe the rumormongers. It's they who have a field day when tearing to shreds the virginal "white gloves" image attached to Grace by the mainstream press in her heyday, and still subscribed to by her most devout fans. Instead, those scandal lovers employ the metaphor coined by Alfred Hitchcock to describe Grace's sexuality, of being a "snow-covered volcano" or as he put it in another, more direct way, Grace Kelly was the most promiscuous woman he'd ever seen.

So, was it sour grapes? Grace was the ultimate Hitchcock blonde and the notorious director tried (and failed) to fashion many other actresses in her image after she set sail for Monaco. It's fair to say he took her marriage to Rainier and the ending of her film career, if not personally, then badly. His silence on the matter speaks volumes! But it's not only Hitchcock who climbed aboard the rumor bus where Grace's love life was concerned. Though the 1950s press followed a more discreet approach than in the twenty-first century, *Confidential* magazine spilled the beans on a number of Grace's alleged liaisons in the early 1950s.

Do time and retrospect confirm the rumors? Possibly. Grace's sometime fiancé, the fashion designer Oleg Cassini, once said: "To be well dressed is a little like being in love." We might continue Cassini's sartorial simile and argue that Grace tried on a fair few dresses, slipped into a few old faithfuls from time to time, and while she loved her wedding dress, it may not have been her favorite. Her love life then, like her wardrobe, was headline grabbing, noteworthy, and—if you prefer the fast-and-loose approach to finding love—inspirational.

We're talking here about Grace's reputation during her Hollywood years, a time when she'd wriggled out from under the thumb of the patriarchal Jack Kelly but was not yet confined by marriage and the Palace of Monaco. As with Snow White, Grace's Prince Charming will come all in good time, but for now let's sneak a peek under the make-believe bedclothes of those early years to discover her first loves, the affairs with her leading men, and then, for a bit of a hoot if we're not *too* exhausted, we'll learn how to flirt à la Grace based on her most playful movie roles.

YOUNG, FOOLISH . . . AND HAPPY?

Over the years, the pop psychologists among us have led Grace fans a merry dance, attributing her love of older, married men to her feelings for her father, Jack Kelly. Now father figures don't come much more austere, repressive, and harder to impress than he. (Remember that sneering Oscar quote?) But the actress Rita Gam, Grace's lifelong friend, puts an end to the idea of Jack being the prototype. On the contrary, with his love of the theater and his intelligent conversation, "Her uncle George was her ideal man."

Before the men came the boys, and Grace's teenage years were much like any other blonde-haired blue-eyed young socialite at the time. She was in high demand, even if she did feel the ugly duckling next to her older sister, Peggy. Many a young man came knocking for Grace and many were given the knock back, according to Margaret Majer Kelly, her mother, who penned a series of features for the press titled "My Daughter Grace Kelly," published shortly before Grace's wedding.

In 1947, at the age of seventeen, when Grace enrolled at the American Academy of Dramatic Arts in New York, she fell in love for the first time: with her acting coach, Don Richardson. Much to the chagrin of Jack Kelly, he was eleven years her senior and Jewish. "The fact I could fall in love with a Jew was beyond them," noted Grace in a letter to a friend. When brought home to Philadelphia to meet the folks, Richardson was given the cold shoulder at an excruciating dinner, a mood that set the precedent for domestic meet and greets for many a suitor to come.

The Richardson romance blew over, and as Grace became a Hollywood hot property, she also became a hot prospect for a date. In the early 1950s she shared an apartment with her sister Lizanne in

New York, and in the autumn of 1953 moved to North Hollywood to live with her friend Rita Gam. At this point she was enjoying playing the dating game but was also involved in a fairly steady relationship with the actor Gene Lyons, her co-star in the TV series *Rich Boy* (1952). But the problem here was that life was imitating art and Lyons, like his character, was a drunk. What's more, he was married, albeit separated. For Grace, a traditional Catholic girl, it was too much; for the Kelly family, more so. But if TV actors brought the stern disapproval of Grace's father, imagine his anxiety when she moved to Hollywood. "I'd like to see Grace married," he told *Time* magazine in 1955. "These people in Hollywood think marriage is a game of musical chairs."

"PRINCESS DISGRACE"

In that same magazine issue, one Hollywood observer is quoted thus: "Wives shouldn't mind if their husbands swoon over [Grace]. Her peculiar talent, you might say, is that she inspires illicit passion." We wonder if this was said with tongue firmly in cheek because at that point in Grace's career, rumor and gossip pursued her with the relentlessness of a particularly ardent lover. Alfred Hitchcock had by 1955 dubbed her "Princess Disgrace" after her alleged affair with *Dial M for Murder* co-star Ray Milland, and as previously mentioned, *Confidential* magazine had already published a number of stories about the young star's *affaires de coeur*.

Wherever Grace went, handsome and obliging men (*and* rumors) seemed to follow her but the woman herself remained tight-lipped on the matter of this Tinseltown tittle-tattle until her dying day. Privacy was important to Grace even before she became a very public princess. How she must have bitten her tongue when that ten-part series about her life and loves was published—*and* penned by her own mother! In fact, the series does not reveal much about Grace's love life. Casting scorn on the rumors of a whole legion of leading men beating down a path to her daughter's (dressing room) door, Margaret Kelly only states that Grace "was involved with at least two of them."

While Margaret Kelly may have been loose-lipped about her daughter's love life, her biographers have been even less restrained, with Robert Lacey and Wendy Leigh both dishing agricultural quantities of dirt in their biographies, *Grace* (1994) and *True Grace* (2007), respectively. Donald Spoto paints a much cleaner picture in his 2010 biography, *High Society*. "The distinct clatter you can hear, as you turn the pages," the *New Yorker* magazine's reviewer writes, "is the sound of skeletons being crammed back into the closet."

COURTING CONTROVERSY

As for our opinion, while we'd love to view Grace's love life with the reverence of her mother, or even with Spoto's Grace-tinted glasses, we can't gloss over the rumors that she is said to have taken the word "close-up" a little too literally with many of her leading men. But was she guilty of love in the third degree in each instance? Let's take her to a Court of Love for a little game of yes, no, maybe so to find out . . .

Gary Cooper

THE ACCUSATION: In Grace's first credited movie role, Cooper (twenty-eight years Grace's senior) is said to have had a private hoedown with his then unknown co-star.

THE EVIDENCE: According to Donald Spoto: "There is not a shred of evidence to support this, or a single reliable source." Wendy Leigh would beg to differ, citing Gary Cooper's friend Robert Slatzer as an authority on the matter. Meanwhile, sister Lizanne, who chaperoned Grace on the set of *High Noon* (1952) at the Kelly family's behest, told biographer James Spada that Grace was infatuated by Cooper.

THE VERDICT: They didn't ride off into the sunset together, but there might well have been a roll or two in the hay bales. So, it's a "maybe so."

Clark Gable

THE ACCUSATION: That, for reasons other than the climate, Kelly and Gable got steamy during the filming of African adventure *Mogambo* (1953). According to legend, Grace then pursued Gable during the filming of the studio shots in London, only to be snubbed by him.

THE EVIDENCE: Actor Donald Sinden, who played Grace's husband in *Mogambo*, recalls stumbling drunkenly into Gable's tent on location only to find the swashbuckling superstar in flagrante delicto with a naked woman. That woman, Sinden suspected, was Grace. Meanwhile, Grace's co-star Ava Gardner later coquettishly neither confirmed nor denied the rumors: "As far as romance went, Clark's eyes were definitely on Gracie, and hers, for that matter, were on him. They were both single at the time and it's very normal for any woman to be in love with Clark."

THE VERDICT: Neither Grace nor Clark fessed up to the affair but the evidence from her co-stars points to a possible "yes." Then there's the disingenuous claims of her mother, who said: "Gracie had more of a schoolgirl crush on Gable than anything else," only to continue this statement by saying the pair were "practically living together." Talk about adding fuel to the flames, Mrs. Kelly! It's a "maybe so."

Ray Milland

THE ACCUSATION: *Confidential* magazine broke the story back in 1954: Grace Kelly was having an affair with the very handsome, very mature, very married Ray Milland, a slice of "action" from the set of *Dial M for Murder* not directed by Hitchcock. The revelation didn't go down too well in Hollywood, not—bizarrely—because of the affair itself, but rather because Grace had been indiscreet about it. What's more, Ray's wife, Mal, was a well-loved Hollywood insider, who was friends with gossip columnist Hedda Hopper.

THE EVIDENCE: Although Milland says he once took her out to dinner, *Time* magazine reported in 1955, "Grace says nothing." Margaret Kelly, meanwhile, acknowledges the rumor: "Grace had put a halt to any affair before it had a chance to get started," but doesn't mention her daughter bringing Milland to the Kelly mansion, where, needless to say, Jack Kelly and co. made the Welsh star feel frostier than a snowman.

THE VERDICT: Dial "Y" for an emphatic "yes!"

Bing Crosby

THE ACCUSATION: It's well documented that the pair had a brief relationship after the death of Crosby's wife, Dixie, during filming of *The Country Girl* (1954). "He was mad about her," said Lizanne. But rumor has it that even before his wife's death, Bing and Grace had used the movie star Alan Ladd's home as a love nest.

THE EVIDENCE: Biographer James Spada claims these trysts in the Ladds' home took place before Dixie's death, just prior to filming for *The Country Girl* began—the information apparently coming from Ladd's wife, Sue, herself.

THE VERDICT: Yes, but whether it was a "single feature" or a "double bill" remains uncertain.

William Holden

THE ACCUSATION: Another double-bill romance, this time during filming of *The Bridges at Toko-Ri* (1954) and possibly also while *The Country Girl* was being filmed.

THE EVIDENCE: The Grimaldi family gave their official approval to Spoto's biography (*High Society*) confirming the affair, where they say Grace "succumbed to the charms of the actor, who was twelve years her senior and married. The friendship rapidly turned into fiery passion."

THE VERDICT: Guilty as charged.

Tony Curtis

THE ACCUSATION: A brief affair during the filming of *The Country Girl* (yes, *another* one!) while Curtis was married to Janet Leigh.

THE EVIDENCE: Curtis himself admits, for the first time, to having had an affair with the "horny Philadelphia girl" in an interview with Kelly's biographer Wendy Leigh.

THE VERDICT: Kelly and Curtis may have liked it hot, but this affair was just a flash in the pan.

Frank Sinatra, Marlon Brando . . . the jury's out on whether we can add these rumored affairs to our list of definite "yes," although there is an affirmative verdict on the Shah of Iran, Prince Aly Khan, and French actor Jean-Pierre Aumont. As Lizanne said: "There was something about her that men just went ape over. It was amazing to see these big names just falling all over themselves" while the girls' mother also acknowledges Grace's charisma: "I was only too aware of the emotions that our Gracie could arouse in men simply by existing."

Oh, to have such charms! And if *we* were so lucky, would we do as Grace did and fall for so many of our leading men? Probably. But like her, doubtless we'd be dreaming of a time when the men we met weren't just available, attractive, and definite A-Listers, we'd be dreaming of that Prince Charming who had that extra je ne sais quoi. Grace's time, as we know, will come, but for now let's leave her in the arms of somebody tall, dark, and handsome as we dim the lights once again for some classic movie moments.

THE GRACE KELLY ACADEMY OF FLIRTING

Illicit passion, affairs, scandal, and rumor . . . Phew! We're already exhausted talking about Grace's love life and that's before we've even gotten to the fictitious flirtations from the movies, whose highlights include a love triangle (or should that be square?), innuendo-laden flirtatious fireworks, and a rumble in the jungle. In fact, in each of Grace's movies there's an abundance of amorous activity that could maybe teach us a thing or two when it comes to the world of dating. Need some seduction instruction? Let's run the videotape then, and see how Grace did it in the following sultry scenes.

Mogambo

THE SCENE: What to do when you fall for an alpha male? (Or, alpha female—the same rules apply.) Here we have Grace in the 1953 colonial jungle romance, playing a bored and buttoned-up anthropologist's wife, who falls for rough and rugged safari guide Victor Marswell (played by Clark Gable). But the problem isn't just her husband, for good-time girl Eloise "Honey Bear" Kelly (Ava Gardner) also wants to get her claws into Gable. Basically, it's a good old-fashioned catfight as to who will land "big cat" Marswell's affections.

THE TECHNIQUE: So, how's a girl to catch her beloved when she's up against raw sex appeal, in this case in the guise of a 5'5" busty brunette? Why, use the time and fairy-tale-tested "Damsel in Distress" routine, of course. In this case Grace's Linda Nordley wanders off into the jungle and falls foolishly into an animal trap; her subsequent rescue by Marswell leads to a passionate act of clothing removal (only a scarf, but hey, it's the fifties!) and an illicit kiss. Unless you live close to a zoo, you'll need to update the "Damsel in Distress" routine for the twenty-first century: fainting, tripping up, or spilling water over your Black-Berry could all be useful modern adaptations of the age-old technique.

THE KILLER PICK-UP LINE: Sadly for la Kelly, Ava Gardner gets all the best lines, while Clark Gable's Marswell has the final word: "Women always fall for the big, white hunter." So this technique comes with a warning: even if you do bag that alpha male/female, be careful of their wandering eye.

Rear Window

THE SCENE: It's that age-old problem: how do you get a man to commit? Here we have Jimmy Stewart playing veteran news photographer, confirmed bachelor, and general commitment-phobe L. B. "Jeff" Jeffries, paired with glamorous Grace as his long-suffering girlfriend, Lisa Carol Fremont. We all know the details of the main plot concerning a possible murder committed in the apartment blocks opposite Jeff's, but this is little more than a classic Hitchcock McGuffin, a vehicle for the far more captivating story of Lisa and Jeff's romance. Throughout the movie, as Jeff attempts to ensnare the killer, Ms. Lisa Fremont does likewise with her man, outwitting him at each and every turn.

THE TECHNIQUE: For the clever ones among you! Here, Grace Kelly's Lisa uses her wit and guile not only to help solve a murder but also to solve the problem of the man who won't commit. In the end her dogged pursuit of the killer wins out, and in a parallel move she wins over Jeff, too.

THE KILLER LINE: One of Grace's best-loved on-screen moments is when she appears in front of Stewart in a negligee, murmuring: "A preview of coming attractions." Take note, blabbermouths: subtlety is *so* much more alluring.

To Catch a Thief

THE SCENE: How to bed a bad boy. Filmed on location near the principality of Monaco, *To Catch a Thief* is the hopeless romantic's dream. Frances Stevens, a bored American socialite holidaying in the South of France with her mother, suspects their new acquaintance, an American industrialist, of being the notorious cat burglar, John Robie (Cary Grant). Flirtation, interrogation, and titillation ensue.

THE TECHNIQUE: Lay it out there on the table; don't hold back! Francie dangles her jewels and a lot more in front of Robie, who at first refuses to yield to temptation. That this movie came after the Breen era in the Hays Code was a godsend to Hitchcock: euphemism, sexual chemistry, and innuendo between Kelly and Grant abound.

THE KILLER LINE: In one innuendo-laden scene, purporting to be about burglary, Grant and Kelly kiss against a climactic firework display as she mutters: "Ever had a better offer in your whole life?" In other words, don't sell yourself short if you're playing the long game in love.

High Society

THE SITUATION: It's the classic scenario of the love triangle, or in this case, square: what's a girl to do when she has not one, not two, but *three* men snapping at her heels and finding her "sensational"? In one of her most fun and flirtatious roles, Grace plays socialite Tracy Samantha Lord, who faces the enviable dilemma of choosing between the romantic ex-husband (Bing Crosby), the wise-cracking new boy on the block (Frank Sinatra), or her betrothed (the steadfast and boring option), played by John Lund.

THE TECHNIQUE: Unusually Grace plays this one as the ditzy blonde. So, party girl Lord variously bumbles about, flirts her tiny ass off, gets drunk, sings a duet with Crosby, has a midnight dip with Sinatra, and generally—as the song says—has a swell party.

THE KILLER LINE: "I'm such an unholy mess of a girl." Like it or not, sometimes letting loose is the most successful method of ensuring potential suitors form a line down the street. Or you could always try the more vulnerable: "I feel quite small, put me in your pocket," which does the trick with Frank Sinatra on this occasion.

DO IT WITH GRACE OR DISGRACE?

That Grace had such a rich and fulfilling love life is all the more surprising, given the strict moral code attached to romancing in the mid-1950s. Dating was a fairly new phenomenon at the time, coinciding with the rise of that now ubiquitous breed: the teenager. For the first time young people had a little freedom and a little money in their pockets. Put the two together and what did you get? Boys and girls going out on dates unchaperoned and a set of rules for dating so strict you'd think that Grace's parents had written them.

Society as a whole was still very reserved when it came to courting, and this is reflected in dating and sex on the silver screen. Although euphemism and innuendo abound in Grace's movies, most of the content had to adhere to the industry's moral code, the Motion Picture Production Code (otherwise known as the Hays Code), and the following guidance: "No picture shall be produced which will lower the moral standards of those who see it." From 1953 to 1954 Joseph Breen was head of the code and an exceptionally eagle-eyed censor who frustrated actors, writers, and directors alike when he took his red pen to the scripts he deemed risqué. (Making Grace's foray in a negligee for *Dial M for Murder* all the more daring . . .)

Grace, then, and her "more is more" approach to dating appears to have been at odds with social mores of the time. Her stardom and that move away from the Kelly home gave her the freedom to experiment, and her beguiling beauty meant she had to beat off men with a stick. But which approach to dating suits *you* best? Are you sweet as apple pie, following a strict set of rules straight from the pages of a 1950s dating book, or, like Grace, do you have your fingers in many pies, tasting many flavors before choosing a favorite? Not sure? Well, take a look at rules A and B opposite to discover which one is more your style.

A	*B*
Boys should ask girls out and never the other way around.	Not backward about coming forward, you think if you want to bag a special someone, you should let them know it.
Necking (erotic activity above the neck) is permissible on a first date.	Anything goes on a first date. There's a story that when her acting teacher Don Richardson first visited Grace's apartment, she came out of the bedroom and surprised him in the nude! (He'd only stopped by for a cup of coffee. . . .)
Petting (erotic activity below the neck) is only permitted when "going steady."	See above!
"Going steady" means you are faithful to one partner, and a sign that you want to take things further.	Until you've got a ring on your finger (and even when you have), you prefer to keep your options open, just as Grace did.
Keep your sexuality under wraps.	Flounce about in a negligee (see *Rear Window* and *Dial M for Murder*). Though you might want to take care with this one—look what happened to our Grace in the latter when she gave the see-through look a go.

All As? Congratulations! You'd be right at home in the etiquette minefield of 1950s dating. All Bs? Why, when it comes to romance, you're the very incarnation of Ms. Grace Patricia Kelly! But perhaps you're somewhere in between? That probably makes you quite normal, and free to enjoy the best of both worlds.

*J*oking aside, what can we learn from Grace here? Well, no matter what the so-called rules of dating of your peers and culture, you should almost certainly break them. Follow your own intuition, lose your inhibitions, and most of all, have plenty of fun! And if you change your mind about your approach to *amour*, who cares? So long as you learn from your mistakes along the way, it's nobody's business but your own.

FASHIONING A FIANCÉ

"We were in love. We were engaged to be married.
That is the truth. No more, no less."

OLEG CASSINI

Even so, there comes a time in every girl's life—even a Hollywood superstar's—when she wants to find that special someone. But up until 1954 there had been no king to sit beside the Queen of Hollywood on her throne. Step up the first pretender to that crown, fashion designer Oleg Loiewski Cassini, who, after Gene Lyons, was the first beau to make Grace think seriously about committing.

The twists and turns of Grace and Oleg's relationship could have come straight from the pages of a romantic novel. Their first meeting came just after Oleg had seen Grace play Linda Nordley in *Mogambo*, only to find her dining with a friend in a New York restaurant that very same night. After proclaiming to his friend: "This girl is going to be mine!" he pursued her ardently, passionately, chasing after her across continents as she headed for France to film *To*

Catch a Thief, and back again to the States when she returned after filming.

Now in 1954 Grace was ready to settle down, it's true. Hard as it may be to believe, she was dissatisfied with her love life at this point, telling *Vogue* in 1972 that despite her professional success, "I didn't have a personal life that was complete." So when a proposal of marriage came, even if it was a lukewarm one, Grace was all for it. But she and her new lover had not accounted for a Jack Kelly–shaped obstacle in the path of their romance. Put plainly, Grace may have succumbed to the charms of the effervescent and persistent Russian but the Kelly clan most certainly did not. Divorced! A non-Catholic! As Margaret Kelly would tell Cassini at a typically frosty luncheon, he might have been "a very charming escort," but he was equally "a very poor risk for a marriage." Brother Kelly would put it less delicately: "I don't generally approve of these oddballs she goes out with," he told *Time* magazine in 1955. Poor flamboyant, foreign-sounding, fashion-conscious Cassini . . . To his pain Grace did not back him up during that difficult luncheon and when her parents asked for a six-month moratorium on the engagement and she did not protest, the game was up.

And within a year's time Grace would be dancing to a very different, and very regal tune, which nobody could have predicted.

chapter four

The Grace Kelly Look

"The thing that made her stand out is what we call 'style.'"
MCCALL'S MAGAZINE, 1955

JACKIE O, AUDREY HEPBURN, Marilyn Monroe, Princess Diana, Victoria Beckham . . . Move over, darlings! Style icons one and all, you may be, but to our minds Grace beats you hands down to the number-one spot in history's role call of fashion's leading ladies. Sure, Audrey had the Capri pants and Jackie O had the glasses, but only Grace has given her name to an entire look. Take a bow, Grace Patricia Kelly, for today we are handing you an imaginary, but heartfelt, (pearl-studded) medal for your eponymous "Grace Kelly Look."

In this chapter we'll raise the underskirts of "The Look" for a sneakier peek into the secrets of Grace's wardrobe. What made her style so distinctive? Who were her favorite designers? How did she go from being the all-American girl to wearing haute couture with such dash and panache as Grace, Princess of Monaco? Here, you'll find the answers to all these questions and more.

To tempt you further, we'll also explore how you can capture Grace's innate sense of style and sophistication simply by introducing a number of key items into your wardrobe. From her early American "college girl" look of shirtdresses, Capri pants, and pumps to her simple yet glamorous royal trousseau, to her pristine accessories of white gloves and pearls, we put Grace's wardrobe through the fashion wringer and update it for the modern wardrobe, so that by the end of this chapter you'll be a little wiser . . . and a lot more stylish.

But remember, we don't suggest you become Kelly carbon copies: half a century on, wearing "The Look" pearl for pearl, kid glove for kid glove, you may look as if you're in costume: inspiration is what you are aiming for here. Yet, Grace's golden rule of keeping things classically elegant never dates, nor do her principles for good posture and good grooming.

Last, but not least, let's not forget clothes are fun, and it would be a foolish fashionista who becomes a style slave, something Grace certainly wasn't. Despite being a style icon and one of the world's most photographed women, she updated her wardrobe only occasionally and wore favorite items more than once—even for special occasions. So, it's with a pinch of common sense, a dash of style savoir-faire, and a heavy sprinkling of twenty-first-century canniness that we say: on to the clothes.

THE GRACE KELLY STYLE GUIDE

First things first, let's begin with a no-frills (except for a few lace trimmings) guide to Grace's fashion fundamentals.

IF IT AIN'T BROKE, DON'T TRY AND FIX IT (AKA: FIND YOUR LOOK AND STICK WITH IT):

Early on, Grace found a style that suited her. Take these words from a friend going back to her days at the American Academy of Dramatic Arts: "Grace's usual outfit was a sweater or cardigan, a bandana or scarf, simple skirt, and always her glasses—nothing glamorous." These key items of twin set and scarf would become hallmarks of Grace's style. Likewise, the white kid gloves she sported for more formal occasions became a trademark item, setting her apart from the less demure Hollywood starlets of the day. According to Grace's sister Lizanne this was a throwback to childhood when their mother had always insisted her girls wear a hat and gloves whenever they left the house. Not to mention the rules at the girls' convent school, where the nuns were very strict on the matter of appropriate attire.

> *"Fashion fades, only style remains the same."*
> COCO CHANEL

Even though Grace's arrival in Hollywood saw her look take an elegant step further toward the glamorous, she always remained true to this well-groomed style and her rules of simple elegance. Oleg Cassini would later claim in his autobiography that his influence was at play here, and that it was he, in fact, who was the mastermind behind the "Grace Kelly Look." "I put her in subdued, elegant dresses that set off her patrician good looks," he wrote. "I told her that beauty should always be set off like a great diamond, in very simple settings. The focus was always to be on her."

Later, Grace would echo these words in a telling statement where she explains her love of simple, classic clothes: "I have to choose simple clothes because when I wear anything dramatic I seem to get lost." As her fame and fortune grew, she wore not only Cassini's own designs, but quickly assimilated a coterie of further favored designers whose clothes she felt best reflected her style and figure—Helen Rose, Dior, Givenchy, Marc Bohan, and Yves Saint Laurent, among them. This fidelity to certain designers ran parallel to the loyalty that she would show to friends throughout her life.

What we learn from Grace here is to wear what suits you, to find a brand linked to that "Look," and to be prepared to adapt it as your lifestyle and/or fashions change.

WEAR IT WELL

"Grace's luxurious trousseau shows good taste."
PHILADELPHIA INQUIRER, 1956

Grace was renowned for her own immaculate taste as early as 1954, when she was named on America's Best-Dressed List. This is reflected in an article concerning the forty-piece trousseau she would be taking to Monaco that appeared in the *Philadelphia Inquirer* in April 1956. Grace didn't simply wear tasteful clothes, though: she wore them *well*. Her early ambition to be a ballerina, as well as her modeling career, taught her that clothes look so much better when you carry yourself upright. Perfect posture makes for perfect ensembles, so hold your back straight, your head high, and don't cross your legs. ("It makes your legs look fat," Grace once said.)

RIGHT CLOTHES, RIGHT TIME

"Our life dictates a certain kind of wardrobe."
GRACE PATRICIA KELLY

Wearing the right clothes for the right occasion is a key barometer of taste and style. Even Edith Head, Paramount's chief costume designer, once proclaimed: "I have never worked with anybody who had a more intelligent grasp of what we were doing." Remember during the filming of *Dial M for Murder* and Grace's insistence that she wear the sheer negligee rather than a robe/dressing gown in the key botched murder scene? This eye for an outfit was mirrored in real life, where she never made sartorial slip-ups and always knew instinctively when to dress up *and* when to dress down. Her one, and only one, public faux pas being when she wore white to Prince Charles and Lady Diana Spencer's 1981 wedding. Poor Grace! So embarrassed was she by the hurtful comments written about her outfit in the British press that she never wore it again. Apropos that . . .

MAKE DO, MEND, AND WEAR IT AGAIN

"I just buy clothes that take my eye, and I wear them for years."
GRACE PATRICIA KELLY

Improbable though it sounds in this era of overconsumption, Grace wore favored pieces more than once, just like the Duchess of

Cambridge—even in the public eye. But let's not put too fine a point on it: she also had the occasional urge to splurge. (She was a millionaire movie star, after all.) While shopping with Edith Head in Paris for the costumes for *To Catch a Thief* (1955), Grace splurged on such indulgent quantities of her trademark Hermès gloves that she had to send for more money. Nevertheless, her usual shopping strategy was to buy what suited her and wear it time and again. Perhaps she was following these wise words from Coco Chanel: "Elegance does not consist in putting on a new dress."

ACCESSORIZE, ACCESSORIZE, ACCESSORIZE

We've covered what have been termed the "inevitable white gloves" but gloves aside accessories were crucial to accenting Grace's simple look. She was also known for her headscarves, strings of white pearls, and her sunglasses, as well as that ubiquitous "Kelly bag." An example of Grace using accessories to great effect was the jewelry she wore at the announcement of her engagement to Prince Rainier. An elegant champagne-colored three-quarter-length-sleeved shirtdress in a rich fabric was offset beautifully by a small gold brooch, gold earrings, and a chiffon scarf around her neck. The message is clear: put the same care and attention into your accessories as you do your clothes, and some of that old Grace magic may just rub off.

THE KELLY BAG

"Handbags are major markers of personal style."

CHRISTA WEIL

It's the Kelly bag that is the accessory most sartorially synonymous with Grace and her "Look." She was often spotted (and inevitably photographed) with an Hermès handbag in the mid-1950s—for instance, at the 1955 Cannes Film Festival and in 1956 at the announcement of her engagement. Later, in 1956, legend has it she used the bag to discreetly cover her baby bump from prying paparazzi. Grace not only gave birth to her first born, Princess Caroline, but to a new trend—this style of bag was thereafter known as a Kelly bag.

Somewhat bulky compared to modern handbags, the Kelly bag is rectangular, almost briefcase-like, modeled on the saddlebags of the 1930s. Made of the finest leather and with a strong metal clasp, the bag is—as Grace was—practical, stylish, and yet fundamentally exclusive.

So, for a sure-fire instant "Gracification" of your wardrobe, it makes sense to get your mitts on one. But there's a catch. Only a limited number of these handcrafted items are made each year, leading to an eye-watering price tag of more than a few months' salary. We don't want to make assumptions, but if you're anything like us, your with-luck-soon-to-be-Kelly-purse strings won't run to a new model. Fear not, handbag hankerers, there are a number of ways you can aim for the same look without the prohibitive price tag.

GO VINTAGE: There are a plethora of vintage specialists, flea markets, thrift shops, not to mention that great virtual second-hand shop eBay, where you may get hold of an authentic vintage item (though these can also go for as much as $4,000). If you do go down this route, take note of the following top tips to ensure you get the bargain, not the fake, of the century:

⊙ Check that the stitching is small, regular, and even (although the seam will be sewn at an angle in an authentic Hermès)

⊙ Listen for the heavy metal clasp "clunking" shut

⊙ Check inside the bag for an embossed Hermès logo

⊙ Feel the leather to check the quality; your nose can be a guide here too

⊙ In a real Hermès, as with all expensive bags, the lining will be silk or suede

REPLICAS

While this may not be the most ethical route (Grace herself was not one for knockoffs), let's get real: Hermès is not about to go out of business if you visit one of the many online replica sites for your Kelly bag. (Remember, you get what you pay for, so don't expect quality.) On the UK main street, stores such as Primark often carry their own brand versions of classic bags while in both the UK and the US, TJ Maxx is always worth a try for your Kelly bag copy.

DIY

Failing this, you could always try the hands-on approach and download the pattern for the Kelly bag from the Hermès Web site. OK, so the pattern is for a mini paper version of your coveted item, but you can always sit and pine while gazing at it, dreaming of the day when you can actually afford the real thing. And that's Grace Handbag Style in the bag.

THE GRACE KELLY CAPSULE WARDROBE

The advent of *Mad Men* has been a godsend for Grace devotees, with high fashion following the lead of the top designers for Kelly Look–inspired items. We'll provide the lowdown on where you can source such items in a bit, but first, a list of your Kelly capsule wardrobe must-haves.

SCARVES: Grace had an abundance of scarves that she wore to accent her outfits, or wrapped around her head to wear with sunglasses. So closely associated with scarves is she, in fact, that a scarf knotted under your chin is known as a "Grace Kelly."

SUNGLASSES: Wayfarer sunglasses and retro styles are key accessories for Grace fans—think *To Catch a Thief* or her jet-setting tours of Europe for your inspiration.

JEWELRY: Pearls are a girl's best friend in Grace's world, but for modern gals, and for subtlety, we don't suggest you go all out with an earrings, bracelet, and necklace combo.

COLLEGE-GIRL CLOTHING: Shirtdresses with cinched waists, Capri pants, and cardigans worn with ballet flats are essential for your wardrobe's retro revamp.

TAILORED SUITS AND TWIN SETS: For more formal occasions and/or work, twin sets can be updated when teamed up with modern pieces or worn in modern colors.

EVENING GOWNS: The dresses worn by Grace in *High Society* and *Rear Window* ought to provide ample inspiration: choose from long Grecian-style to full-skirted, mid-length 1950s-style gowns, or even that masquerade gold ball gown in which Grace wowed audiences in *To Catch a Thief*. And although it's for her costumes as a movie actress and her 1950s wardrobe that we love her most, we can't omit Grace's maxi coats and maxi dresses from the 1970s as other must-have items, if the longer look floats your boat.

That's all well and good, you might think; I know what to wear, but where do I get it? Fret not. Here's a mini guide to your wardrobe's Kelly conversion:

DESIGNER:

○ **Prada.** Look no further for the ultimate designer sundress.

○ **Hermès.** For scarves, gloves, and bags.

○ **Salvatore Ferragamo.** Scarves, eyewear, and handbags with a nod to the Kelly Look.

○ **Lulu Guinness.** For fun and frivolous 1950s-inspired shoes and handbags.

○ **Chanel.** If you can afford it, your first stop for a tailored suit.

○ **Ghost.** Grecian-inspired evening wear, such as the Helen Rose dress Grace wore in *High Society*.

○ **Ray-Ban.** Classic Wayfarer sunglasses manufacturer.

ON MAIN STREET:

○ **Bloomingdale's.** This old faithful, which has increasingly more stores across the United States (and an excellent online shop), is top-notch for cardigans, sweaters, and other knits.

○ **J.Crew/Ann Taylor.** Both of these upmarket stores carry cardigans and twin sets, and generous lines in supersoft cashmere offer us mere mortals the chance to experience some Grace-like luxury every day.

○ **Online.** The Internet—so much more convenient at times than the actual main street—offers ample opportunity to find vintage looks. At the top of our list is www.shopruche.com, a vintage-inspired boutique with a modern touch, its 1950s look book "inspired by classiness and sophistication." We hardly need remind you whose image these words should conjure up. At the more sultry starlet end of the spectrum, sites such as www.bettiepageclothing.com offer the classic fifties sweater and pencil-skirt silhouette and fun, frivolous party wear. Last but not least is www.modcloth.com, which carries collections such as Emily and Fin, a British design team that offers a lovely range of 1950s-shaped day dresses.

VINTAGE:

Clearly, vintage shops are your best bet if it's a truly authentic look you are seeking. There are numerous vintage Web sites online, but we recommend shopping in the old-fashioned way for your old-fashioned look—true vintage vultures know that only by trying on a garment can you know if it fits perfectly. If you can sew (or know someone who can), for the perfect fit and an authentic look, try vintage patterns. *Vogue* carries a line of replica vintage patterns (including wedding gowns), while eBay is a vintage pattern paradise, where you can do no worse than hunt down the McCall "Easy Sew" dress worn by Grace when she first met Prince Rainier. Happy shopping!

SUNGLASSES TO HIDE BEHIND

Being one of the world's most photographed women, Grace often hid behind her shades. She wore them so often, it was vital she found a style that suited her face: opting for the classic Wayfarer Ray-Bans (first around in 1952), which were perfect for her strong jawline. If, like Grace, you want to look your best in your summer eyewear, here is a short section on choosing the right sunglasses for your face.

First and foremost, sunglass size should be in scale with your face size. If you have a small face, go for smaller glasses (and vice versa for larger faces). The shape of the frame should be opposite to your face shape, such as:

• SQUARE. If, like Grace, you have a strong jawline, you need to rid yourself of those angles, so go for cat-eye styles. Classic ovals and round styles will also work for you.

• OVAL. Lucky you, most styles suit this shape so the sunny sky's the limit for you oval-faced lovelies!

• ROUND. Wider frames with angular/rectangular styles help your face look longer and thinner.

• TRIANGULAR. Having a narrow jaw and a wide forehead, or a "triangle face" lends itself well to frames with a straight top line or cat-eyes.

• HEART-SHAPED. Many styles work for the heart-shaped face: just be careful your sunglasses are not too wide to bring attention to your narrow chin. (Aviators could be a good look on you.)

And remember, your complexion will look different depending on which frame you choose: those with pale complexions should avoid darker frames, olive complexions suit metallic and light tortoiseshell frames, while dark and black complexions look best in metallic frames. Dark-rimmed sunglasses, although *very* Hollywood, can be tricky for most complexions—you have been warned!

ICE, ICE BABY

"Grace brought a balance back to Hollywood between femmes fatales and pin-ups."

FRÉDÉRIC MITTERRAND

We couldn't leave you thinking you'd got Grace's look down pat without including some advice on emulating one last aspect of her style, something that set her apart from other movie stars of the day and had many a male co-star hot under the collar. That is, the effect of her cool, reserved way of dressing, coupled with a simmering, if sublimated, sexuality; together Sir Alfred Hitchcock called this her "sexual elegance." In other words, if you've got it, flaunt it, lady! But be sure to do so with an understated sensuality that'll have him eating out of your hand. Not that everybody was keen on Grace's ice maiden credentials. In fact, *Vogue* magazine went so far as to say in January 1955 that she was "too wholesome to be mysterious" and to dub her "as remote as a snow queen."

They were missing a trick. Grace's reserved manner of dressing in cardigans, glasses, gloves, and hats endeared her not only to the general public but also to the English film director Alfred Hitchcock. In his compelling 1983 book, leading director of the French nouvelle vague François Truffaut discusses Grace Kelly's "indirect sex appeal" with Hitchcock, who puts it this way: "Sex on screen should be suspenseful. If sex is blatant or too obvious, there's no suspense." Small wonder then, Hitchcock's preference for ice-cool Grace over the more overtly sexual stars of the day: Marilyn Monroe, Jane Russell, and Grace's close friend Ava Gardner. Hitchcock plays this to great effect in *To Catch a Thief*. As we meet Frances Stevens we see her as Hitchcock describes it: "classical, beautiful, and very distant." But then, wham, bam! When Cary Grant walks her to her hotel room, she catches him off-guard with a lingering, sexually charged kiss. The (white) gloves are off: underneath the ice maiden is a smoldering sex goddess.

GET THE ICE MAIDEN LOOK

With a few key touches you can adapt Grace's sensuous elegance to the twenty-first-century wardrobe. Hey, no one's suggesting you go all out in veils, gloves, and other such hangovers of a more polite and more formal bygone era, but still the principle of "less is more" will stand you in good seductive stead. Just remember: smuttiness and slovenliness are out; gentility and good grooming are in.

○ Necklines and hemlines should be high and low, respectively.

○ Daywear should include tailored items: for an up-to-date look, try shorts (daring to bare legs in summer, with opaque tights in the winter months).

○ In the evening, don't go bust (ahem!) for plunging décolletage. Try a vintage gown with a brooch, albeit with heels. And forget the white gloves (unless it's black tie).

○ Learn to love lace: it's recently made a comeback as a major fashion item. Grace wore it both in her movies (who can forget *that* red lace dress when we first see her with her lover in *Dial M for Murder?*) and in real life: her wedding dress and civil ceremony suit both draped our leading lady in lace.

And let's not forget there is nothing less sexy than taking oneself too seriously (Grace didn't). Her biographer Wendy Leigh cites several instances of Grace using naked (both senses of the word) surprise to woo her suitors (remember Don Richardson from the last chapter?). Take Robert Saltzer, who tells Leigh that, on their first date back at his place, "Grace immediately went into the bathroom, then came out stark naked." Who needs clothes when there's your ultimate weapon— your body? If this lays things a little too, ahem, bare, take a leaf out of Lisa Fremont's book (Grace's character in *Rear Window*) as she prances about in her negligee. Coquette Kelly would almost certainly have enjoyed acting that particular piece of quietly seductive celluloid.

THE WEDDING GOWN OF
THE CENTURY

It would be unthinkable to discuss Grace's style without mentioning one of her defining moments as a true goddess of style: her transformation from Hollywood Queen to Monaco's Princess. The law in Monaco required that Grace and Prince Rainier had both a civil and a religious marriage ceremony. Lucky Grace! This meant two outfits, each reflecting her personality and style in entirely different ways.

For the civil ceremony, on April 18, 1956, Grace wore an elegant suit designed by MGM's head costume designer, Helen Rose. A dusty silk rose color with a fitted bodice and full skirt, the suit was of taffeta and lace. The outfit was finished off with a small hat and of course Grace's trademark white gloves.

The following day, April 19, Grace wore another Helen Rose–designed gown. And what a gown it was: the lace bodice referenced the previous day's civil ceremony outfit, while the skirt was an opulent ivory silk affair with a high cummerbund and full train. Grace's hands were bare, her heart was on her sleeve: she was marrying her Prince Charming. Reporters at the time referred to Grace's wedding gown as her co-star, while later Vera Wang described the dress as both "majestic" and "demure"—no mean feat! Over fifty years later, the legacy of the dress lives on: when Catherine Middleton married Prince William in April 2011, her wedding dress of silk and lace was a nod to Grace's stunning and, dare we say, more spectacular gown from 1956.

GRACE STYLE Q & A

I have a blind date planned for this weekend. Should I dress to impress? I hear this one's quite a catch so I want to look my seductive best.

Come now, have you been listening? Sophisticated, not slutty, is the way forward to capture your best beloved's heart. When Grace met Prince Rainier for the first time in 1956 (and despite some teething problems with an iron and humidity), she got the outfit spot-on, festooning herself in a black floral day dress styled from a McCall's pattern—square necked and with a full skirt—while her hair was set in an updo, with a floral headpiece bringing a soft, feminine touch. Naturally, the outfit was finished off with white kid gloves. Bringing this up-to-date, no one's suggesting you drape yourself from head to toe in chintz. But do take a leaf (or rather, *flower*) out of Grace's book: go for something elegant and feminine to do the trick, such as a floral dress or a flower in your hair (men seem to like this and if you're gay, she'll appreciate the effort), pretty shoes, and a matching bag.

I've been invited to a black-tie event but I can't afford a new dress. There's an old favorite calling me fondly from the back of the wardrobe but shouldn't I go for something shiny and new?

We repeat: in the post-war years and the era of make do and mend, sporting a garment once, twice, or three times (and beyond) was no fashion faux pas. Just think of the gorgeous silvery blue satin gown Grace wore like a second skin during her 1955 Oscar acceptance speech for *The Country Girl*; the same garment had been on display to the world a year previously at the premiere of the very same film. The message is clear: if the frock fits, wear it (be sure it's freshly dry-cleaned), and you will be the belle, not to mention budgeter, of the ball.

All this is well and good, but I'm not sure I take clothes that seriously. I'm no style icon.

That's OK. Grace applied her usual common sense and love of life to clothes. "I think it is important to see the person first and the clothes afterward," she is often quoted as saying. And let's not forget, despite the haute couture of later years, the memorable wedding dress, and the closet full of designer frocks, it's for her simple, laid-back college-girl style that Grace is best remembered. Her son, Prince Albert II of Monaco, has said of her innate sense of style and sophistication: "Throughout her life, she exuded effortless elegance, whether she was appearing at a special occasion or at a simple family gathering." Elegance may be important, but effortlessness equally so.

MOVIE MAKEOVER

Throughout this chapter, your sartorial synthesis with Grace's wardrobe has come with a warning: don't overdo it! We've said it once and we'll say it again, what we've been grounding you in here is inspiration based on the Grace Kelly Look, not a mirror image of Grace down to the last buttonhole. That said, black-tie wear sometimes does have its place—at black-tie parties, of course! So, to conclude our musings on the Grace Kelly Look, we're going to lighten the mood a little and invite you to a black-tie affair, taking our Grace Kelly–style school to a whole new level with some more direct ideas for reproducing key looks from a selection of the movies:

GET THE *HIGH NOON* LOOK

If you want to copy the fashions from this early picture of Grace's, start by thinking in sepia tones, then add a frilly bonnet and sturdy ankle books. And, although Grace's character was a demure Quaker, if pious doesn't suit your coloring, there's no reason not to cast your net wildly and think Wild West saloon girl more in keeping with Katy Jurado in the same picture. So, how about some frilly petticoats and a flippy tiered skirt?

Don't forget a tiny (fake!) pistol in your décolletage.

GET THE *MOGAMBO* LOOK

Think *Out of Africa* style. In the movie Grace is clad in khakis and safari suits. As this was an early color picture, apply some bright red lipstick to show off the new technology to the hilt.

GET THE *DIAL M FOR MURDER* LOOK

It's got to be that chiffon nightgown. The key here is that, though the gown was daringly sheer, it also grazed the floor. Of course it famously rode up in the fight-for-life scene. Yours might ride up too, in the right thrilling moment—though hopefully it won't be a matter of life and death!

GET THE *REAR WINDOW* LOOK

Grace's look in this movie is the one we most associate with her everyday style. The perfectly pressed and tailored fifties clothes, the white gloves, and the pillbox hats. And what about those Edith Head–designed gowns?

To embody classic Grace, track down precise vintage wear, Chanel-style suits, twin sets, tight sweaters, and pencil skirts, and above all, make sure you are always immaculately turned out, with ne'er a crease or scuff to be found.

GET THE *COUNTRY GIRL* LOOK

One word: cardigan. If any single garment sums up Grace's somewhat dowdy look in this film, it's her oversized, sloppy cardigan. *The Country Girl* look is the one ensemble where you can dress in your slouchiest clothes and still claim to be channeling la Grace!

GET THE *TO CATCH A THIEF* LOOK

Go wild with Capri pants, tie elegant scarves around your perfectly styled hair, and sport stripy T-shirts for that fifties French vibe. Once again, red lipstick is a must. If you can run to the open-top car and tempt a Cary Grant look-alike along for the ride, so much the better! Or, if you dare to bare, you could do no worse than sport some playful yellow-skirted swimwear and white-rimmed sunglasses— nothing says Riviera chic more.

GET THE *HIGH SOCIETY* LOOK

Too much is simply not enough for this one. As rich, mon-eyed Tracy Samantha Lord, Grace exuded wealth and status. Think Christian Dior's New Look, with enormous starchy full skirts and kitten heels. Or for the ultimate *High Society* look, ask a seamstress to replicate Lord's de-lightful pink/gray embroidered evening gown designed by Helen Rose. Style your hair in loose blonde curls and then pose on the nearest veranda, cocktail in hand.

chapter five

Ice-Cool Beauty

"I think I'm quite nice looking but that's about it."

GRACE PATRICIA KELLY

A KEY FACTOR IN THE durability of Grace Kelly's legacy is her looks. Fresh-faced, natural, and lovely, Grace has features that we can look at time and again without tiring. She has an expressive, adaptable face that doubtless helped her win all those countless plaudits and acting awards. Whether channeling Gary Cooper's "fair-haired beauty" Quaker wife in *High Noon*, sensational blonde bombshell Tracy Lord in *High Society*, or the downbeat, grittily determined Georgie Elgin in *The Country Girl*, Grace gave good—and talented—face.

Unusually for the flirtatious fifties, her beauty was sophisticated and understated. She stood out from the crowd without resorting to self-promotion by prancing about scantily clad or wearing "falsies," eyes weighted down by ludicrously long false lashes; no slatternly sexpot was she, posing for "cheesecake" photos like so many of her peers. As her favored photographer Howell Conant said: "You trusted Grace's beauty; you knew it was not built from clothes and makeup." It's a girl-next-door look, whose wholesomeness helped her win all those modeling contracts at the start of her career.

What Grace also brought to the (beauty) party of the 1950s was a seductive but sophisticated appeal, which had her pinned as both a great beauty and an ice queen. It also had the newspapers of the day eating out of her white-gloved hand. The *Sarasota Journal* waxed lyrical over Grace's looks in 1954, saying: "She's blonde, blue-eyed, cool, composed, and cultured," while the *Ottawa Citizen* was equally flattering a year later, calling her "a cool and collected refined beauty." Both papers refer to Grace's perfect poise, pristine manners, and good grooming as key qualities of the rising star.

This daring to be different from the sultry starlets of the day stood Grace in good stead throughout her entire movie career, and although becoming a princess brought out her softer, warmer side, she never deviated from the elegantly cool allure for which she was feted in the fifties. In this chapter we'll give a few hints and tips on how you too can capture Grace's ice-cool look, her enviable figure, and perfectly peachy skin. We'll then go on to examine what it takes to become a blonde bombshell, how to disguise your worst features, and how the time-pressed modern female can cheat her way to good grooming. In short, we'll pull out our (makeup) bag of tricks to answer the question: when it comes to spending time in the beauty parlor, what would Grace do?

VITAL STATISTICS

"All women really want the same thing: to look like themselves,
only prettier and more confident."

BOBBI BROWN, MAKEUP GURU

Before we delve into the nitty-gritty, or rather *pretty* gritty, of beau-
tifying yourself à la Grace, let's press pause to ponder the basics of
her enviable natural loveliness. Irish and German descent gifted
Grace with her chiseled features, strong jawline, and of course, those
mesmerizing blue eyes. With athleticism running in the family (her
mother, Margaret, was a competitive swimmer and her father an
Olympic sculler), it's no mystery how Grace came to be in posses-
sion of such a slender to-die-for figure. What does remain a mystery
is just how slender she was, for, like her cleavage, Grace kept her
vital statistics under wraps throughout her entire life. The World-
Wide Web confidently asserts her measurements to be 34-24-35,
and the photos and movies certainly don't call this into serious
question, but since the lady herself remained buttoned up on the
matter, we cannot say for sure. What we do know is that she stood
proudly (no humpbacked huncher was she) at 5'7" tall and is said
to have worn the smallest dress size of the time: a US 10.

Keeping her weight down did not come easily, though. In 1954
Grace told a journalist that she had to work hard to stay slim and
rode horses, swam, and played tennis in order to keep her figure, as
well as going on the occasional diet. A year later, a famous 1955
Time magazine article, "The Girl in White Gloves," about Grace at
the peak of her fame, cites: "Four times a week she puts her hair into
a ponytail, dons a leotard, and goes off to classes in modern dancing
and ballet." According to her biographer Robert Lacey, this commit-

ment to her physique lessened as she grew older, and her diet in later life was not so great. (Can you blame her, living amid the temptation of croissants, mille-feuilles, and royal chefs?)

Grace's 1972 interview with *Vogue* goes some way to backing up this theory, with the princess confirming she was no longer dieting or exercising. Looking at the photos of Grace by Lord Snowdon that accompany the article, her beauty nevertheless still shines through. Dressed in an elegant pink gown, her eyes sparkling with intelligence, the skin dewy and porcelain-doll-like, Grace, at forty-two, was still one of the world's most beautiful women. So she'd put on a few pounds, but we admire her all the more for not being a slave to her figure her entire life—goodness knows she'd worked hard enough in the 1950s! Not that she had ever kowtowed to the gods of fashion or had been a slave to her looks. That she looked so good most of the time was a natural blessing and was never down to an entourage of primpers and preeners. In everyday life she was her own wardrobe mistress and she had always done her own hair and makeup. Even while residing at the palace in Monaco she only brought in makeup artists and hairdressers for special events.

Of course it was easy for Grace: with her chiseled chin, small brow, flashing blue eyes, and blonde hair, the beauty fairy had been more than generous the day she was born. And it was her blonde hair and blue eyes that saw her in high demand during her early modeling career, as a Hitchcock blonde and a much photographed princess. It was also those features that attracted her husband, Prince Rainier. For a final word on the matter let's hand the mike over to him, as he described Grace to a friend when they were courting. Grace, he said, "is a blonde girl with that sort of beauty that grows on you, with long floating hair and eyes of blue."

BARE-FACED BEAUTY

"Achieving the appearance of radiant and truly healthy skin is always a goal for me. I feel prettiest when I am confident about my skin."

CHRISTY TURLINGTON, SUPERMODEL

Studying photos of Grace, from that 1955 *Time* magazine cover to Snowdon's cover shot for *Vogue* in 1972, what leaps off the page is that in nearly twenty years, Grace's flawless skin tone had barely succumbed to the ravages of time. Sure, we can't all be blessed with such perfectly peachy cheeks, but with a few basic changes we can improve skin tone and color. Eating well, drinking water, and—*do* excuse the capitals, but it's important—NOT SMOKING will leave us happier and more glowing in the skin we live in. (As an aside, Grace never did smoke. In films where her characters smoked, clever angles and cutaways were used, so although her character might be seen to be holding a cigarette, or stubbing one out, she most definitely did not inhale.)

MAKEUP BAG OF TRICKS

Sometimes lifestyle and bad habits get in the way of our best intentions, though, and that's when it's time to splash the cash and acquire a few beauty cult classics, of which the following are our tried and tested favorites:

CLARINS BEAUTY FLASH BALM. Applied under your usual foundation or tinted moisturizer, this balm gives skin a lift and instant radiance. We wouldn't advise using the product on its own, though, or skin can look very greasy.

YVES SAINT LAURENT TOUCHE ÉCLAT. The old faithful concealer discreetly covers dark rings under the eyes, as well as shadows around the nose and mouth. Be sure to get the correct shade for your skin tone, though, or it may peek through your foundation.

ORIGINS NO PUFFERY. If, like Grace, you are partial to the occasional tipple, this cooling gel will soothe your under-eye post-party puffing (try saying that after a few!). A small amount can be used for all-day wear, or if you have five minutes, a big dab under each eye will teach those naughty puffed-up bags a thing or two.

BENEFIT BENETINT. For a flirty 1950s flush, apply a *tiny* amount (you want it to look natural) of this liquid to each cheek and rub, rub, rub! High Beam from the same cosmetics line can be added on top of makeup as a highlighter, too.

ELIZABETH ARDEN EIGHT HOUR CREAM. It's one of our biggest regrets, and we say so almost seriously, that we discovered this fixing cream late in life. Spots, pimples, zits, whatever you call them, this miraculous little cream clears up minor skin problems almost overnight and can also be used on burns and chapped lips.

TINTED MOISTURIZER. Grace never looked as though her makeup was plastered on with a trowel and neither should you, so for daytime makeup do consider a tinted moisturizer instead of foundation. You don't have to break the bank here (any tinted moisturizer will do), but if you do feel like going for broke, Laura Mercier's line goes on smoothly and evenly.

Sure, these items all come with a price tag but they're beauty favorites one and all. Used sparingly, they will form a great basis for your skin's transformation to movie-star radiance so long as you don't . . . you know what. Do remember also, whatever your urge to splurge on lotions and potions, most skin-care specialists say the biggest enemy of skin and the begetter of wrinkles is the sun, so always wear sunscreen and sunglasses. It's hardly a chore! Besides, this reasoning gives you a good excuse to pamper your peepers and get a hold of some trademark Grace Wayfarers.

NEVER A HAIR OUT OF PLACE

*"Grooming is the secret of real elegance. The best clothes,
the most wonderful jewels, the most glamorous beauty
don't count without good grooming."*
CHRISTIAN DIOR

Now that you're basking in the glow of perfect skin, it's time to get out there and show the world what you've got! But hold on—just before you do, you'd better make sure when your big toe steps out that front door, it's manicured within an inch of its life, just as each hair is perfectly in place and (our personal bugaboo) your top is not accessorized with this morning's breakfast. Because we're fairly certain if you want to be revered as a ladylike beauty akin to our Grace, your number-one priority should be good grooming. Sure, punk and grunge have their place (in the 1970s and 1990s, if you want our opinion), but not for aspiring Grace Kellys. Yes, even with our busy lives, there's no reason why we modern gals can't be as well turned out as our fifties sisters. And it doesn't take much: with a pluck here and a touch-up there, you can be groomed to perfection in little more than a wave of your mascara wand. Looking neat and groomed was a key part of Grace's timeless elegance and this is easy to achieve if you follow a few simple rules:

BOOK THAT MANI-PEDI. Keep your hands and feet perfectly neat. Chipped nail polish or dry patches are complete no-nos for that totally groomed appearance.

SMELL SWEET. Smell *good*! Regular showers or baths and deodorant are a key part of a daily beauty routine. Don't forget that natural fabrics help, too. It's no use being pleasing to the eye but displeasing to the nose.

THE PERFECT FIT. Your clothes should be the right size. Don't squeeze into something that's too small or wear oversized clothes to try and look more petite. Everything you wear should be spotless, and don't forget to plan your outfits well so they coordinate without being too matchy-matchy.

BE SMOOTH. Master the art of ironing your clothes so everything you wear is perfectly pressed. If you're too, *ahem*, pressed for time for this chore, buy cotton jersey and other items that don't require the same effort. Similarly, don't buy dry-clean or hand-wash only items if you don't have the time or will to care for them.

CROWNING GLORY. Your hair should always be clean, shining, and neat. Try an effortless short style or tie it back in an elegant chignon, with any loose ends hair sprayed to keep neat and tidy all day long.

SCENTSATIONAL. Avoid heavy perfumes, like Christian Dior's notorious Poison. Light, elegant fragrances work best and will be noticeable without being overpowering. Pick a perfect scent and wear it always as your signature. Jo Malone, for instance, has a stunning array of evocative individual colognes.

WELL-HEELED. And don't forget your shoes. Well-fitting and scuff-free means you'll be perfect from top to toe. Taking your shoes to the cobblers at the beginning of each season not only makes your shoes last longer, but keeps you walking in Grace's well-heeled footsteps.

SMILE, SMILE, SMILE! Don't underestimate the impact of a beaming smile. Keep your teeth clean, visit your dentist regularly for a polish, and keep your breath supersweet with sugar-free mints (*never* gum unless you want to be mistaken for a giraffe when you open your mouth).

GET UP EARLY. All these little tips rely on having the time to prepare before you face the day. If you're the sort of person who tumbles out of bed at the very last minute (even if it's somebody else's), rethink. An extra half an hour to check that your shirt is ironed and your hair is perfectly styled will be so worthwhile, as it gives you all-day added confidence and you'll love it when people notice the effort you've made. None are time-consuming, and all are vital, if you wish to channel ladylike Grace.

CHECK YOUR LOOK. Now that you've made the effort, don't leave the house without stealing a glance in a full-length mirror. A quick brush of your hair, a brush down of clothes (if you have pets, this goes double for you), and last-minute brush of your teeth will have you picture perfect.

BATTLE OF THE BLONDES

The curator of a recent exhibition in Toronto to celebrate Grace Kelly's enduring cultural influence described her as "the iconic blonde of the 1950s." Fans of a certain bustier, more vampish, and, they would argue, sexier blonde movie star of that time may beg to differ. Taking a trip in our cinematic time machine to visit the era, we'd find the faces of two blondes plastered across billboards, magazine covers, and movie posters—in some cases at the same time. The cover of *Screen Stars* in May 1955, for instance, features both women. One has the headline: "THE MOST TALKED ABOUT GIRL IN HOLLYWOOD" illustrated by a demure blonde in a ladylike silver gown and glittering jewels, while the other is titled: "FRANK! REVEALING!" THE PRIVATE LIFE OF . . . !" Guess who? Well, blonde number one is our Gracie, while the second blonde, whose private life is so intriguing, is none other than the lovely, lusty Marilyn Monroe.

The contrast in these taglines is telling, highlighting a key difference in the public's perception of the two stars. Throughout her career Grace would be described as "ladylike, patrician, icy, demure, classy," while red-blooded Monroe found her name alongside all those naughty "s"s in the dictionary: "sexy," "sultry," "slutty" even. But which one would win a battle of the blondes and be crowned fabulous blonde of the fifties? Let's have a little fun and find out . . .

ROUND ONE: BATTLE OF THE SEX SYMBOLS

Famous for their physiques, both women modeled at the start of their careers, although let's just say the type of modeling Marilyn undertook was the more risqué variety. And here's a key difference between our two blondes: in the late 1940s while Grace was the wholesome all-American girl modeling in ads for bug spray, Marilyn was a pinup girl in magazines with names like *Glamorous Models* and *Cheesecake.* From this point on, Monroe's sexuality was all up-front and in your face: she wore her heart on her sleeve, bras pointy, dresses sparkly and tight. Kelly, on the other hand, kept her sexuality under wraps, or rather beneath those prim white gloves. When it comes to sexuality, then, ding, ding! Round one to Marilyn.

ROUND TWO: PRIVATE LIVES

A difference in style was echoed in our two blondes' private lives. Grace was known to play her cards close to her chest, granting very few interviews (in her early life, at least) or speaking to publicists. "A person has to keep something to herself, or your life is just a layout in a magazine," she told *Time* magazine in 1955. Meanwhile, Marilyn was often interviewed, both in print and on television, and even penned an autobiography, *My Story.* Unthinkable for Grace! But both women knew how to use the press to their advantage. Still, we can't help clinking our glasses a little louder for Grace's more discreet style when it came to the prying press and paparazzi. Round two, then, belongs to Grace.

ROUND THREE: MOVIE MANIA

Glorious Technicolor was the perfect vessel for showing each actress at her brilliant blonde best, with *Gentlemen Prefer Blondes* and *Dial M for Murder* both processed in that format. Marilyn's year was

1953 when three of her best-loved films—*Gentlemen Prefer Blondes*, *How to Marry a Millionaire*, and the downbeat *Niagara*—were released. The following year, 1954, Grace was crowned Hollywood's queen with *Dial M for Murder*, *The Country Girl*, and *Rear Window* all showing on movie screens. At this point both women's images were bound up in their movie roles: Marilyn played a variety of "dumb blondes" so well that she was typecast and misconstrued as such; Grace was the high society gal. Monroe's success with the critics came later than Kelly's, winning her Golden Globe for *Bus Stop* in 1959, when Grace had already walked off with the Oscar for *The Country Girl* (1954). Still, with both blondes trumping all the other actresses of the mid-fifties, we'd have to call their tussle over the Queen of Hollywood's crown a score-draw.

ROUND FOUR: BLONDE AMBITION

Although they share a hair color, in the looks department the two are poles apart: Grace represents natural beauty, while Marilyn (bottle blonde, voluptuous, and cartoon-like) is the ultimate sex symbol. In the wardrobe department, Marilyn's iconic gowns are flirty and revealing (we're thinking of that famous white sundress from *The Seven Year Itch*, or the hot pink clingy evening gown from *Gentlemen Prefer Blondes*), while Grace's best remembered gowns owe more to couture than to cleavage. Shorter than Grace at 5'5½" and curvier, Marilyn's figure cried out to be snapped as the cheesecake pinup, for which she was well known in the forties. In the looks stakes, then, it depends on your taste: if it's cheesecake with a cheeky dollop of sauce on top, then Marilyn wins this one, but if it's a slice of wholesome and elegant pie, it's Grace.

Adding up the scores, looks like it's a draw for our fabulous fifties icons. Indeed, both women cause us to breathe a regretful sigh that Hollywood's heyday is over. A time when it could lay claim to not one but *two* beautiful blondes, who can be celebrated for their individuality and relentless talent. At a time when stars were just that: stars. It's also poignant that both women left Hollywood soon after their heyday, one for the hills of Monaco and her prince, the other for that great cinematic lot in the sky. Marilyn's engagement congratulations sent to Grace proves telling: "So glad you've found a way out of this business."

HOW TO BE A BLONDE BOMBSHELL

"Being blonde is definitely a different state of mind."

MADONNA LOUISE CICCONE

So, you want to call on your inner blonde, whether Grace or Marilyn? Us too! OK, ladies, we know you're not all blondes (natural or otherwise), but being a blonde bombshell is nothing if not an attitude, right? You might have black skin and an Afro, in which case the blonde bombshell in you does not consist of putting on a platinum blonde wig à la Beyoncé, but rather taking your natural looks to their most extravagant. Redhead? Don't be afraid to be just that: a redhead. Forget all that strawberry-blonde nonsense: say it red, say it loud, say it proud! Or if, like your author, you are pale-skinned and a brilliant brunette, make the most of your raven-haired locks and keep them glossy and clean with highlighters and tonal shades instead of dyeing them all colors of the earth.

In short, whatever your DNA, what makes you interesting is *you*. What we're going for here is channeling: "The withering look of a goddess," as Bing Crosby describes Grace's Tracy Lord in *High Society*. Being a blonde bombshell means taking your beauty to its limits, but having a personality and clothing style to match.

THE FIVE BLONDE BOMBSHELL RULES

5 Your hair should be your crowning glory. Keep it shiny, big, and noticeable, no matter what its color. And if you're not a natural blonde, there's nothing more fun than donning a blonde wig for a party, black-tie affair or otherwise, and playing up your blondeness for a night.

4 Red lips are a must, but what a minefield! Reddish-blue tones are best for pale skins, while orange reds simply clash with redheads but work well for warmer tones. The red lipstick Grace wore in *Dial M for Murder*, for example, is perhaps a little too orange for her skin tone, but she rocks it in *Mogambo* with a bright red that looks fabulous against the African dusky backdrop. The trick here is to experiment until you find a red that suits you (our personal favorite being Mac's "Ruby Woo," a red *so* red it turns heads). Which is what a blonde bombshell is looking for, right?

3 Develop the perfect pout. No use having *the* hair and *the* lips if you don't work them! All it takes is a little practice in front of the mirror. Or in front of your children, if you have them. They'll appreciate the comedic value.

2 Exude confidence. Marilyn did so on camera, even when she was struggling with inner turmoil, and Grace's strength of character is what saw her through those battles with MGM and her father, right through to the difficult years in the palace, later on.

1 Being a blonde bombshell does not equate to dumb, stupid, or slutty. Blondes may have more fun, but what made Grace and Marilyn the stars they were was sharp intellect and street-smart attitude, respectively. Which makes us think of the perfect retort to an accusation of dumb blondeness from one superstar blonde: "I'm not offended by all the dumb blonde jokes because I know I'm not dumb and I also know that I'm not blonde." Well said, Queen of Country Music, Ms. Dolly Parton.

And as a final note on all things blonde, we'd like to point out that Audrey Hepburn, another contender to the Queen of Hollywood's crown, dyed her hair with blonde tones for the part in *Breakfast at Tiffany's*. Which just goes to show even the most brunette of brunettes sometimes just has to go blonde. And who'd have thought Audrey was a "fair lady" in more ways than one?

THE "TOO CATEGORY"

Believe it or not, when Grace started out neither she nor some of her contemporaries considered her to be the great beauty she's acknowledged as being today. Recalling her failed screen test for the movie *Taxi* and director Gregory Ratoff's reaction to this (he wanted her for the part but was overruled by studio bosses), Grace said: "I was in the 'too' category for a very long time. I was too tall, too leggy, too chinny. I remember that Mr. Ratoff kept yelling, 'She's perfect, what I love about that girl is that she's not pretty.' "

Not pretty?

It just goes to show the truth in that old adage about beauty and the eye of the beholder. In another interview, later in her life, Grace herself said:

I've never thought of myself as pretty, though I love it when people pay me compliments. When I was young, I was so bland no one ever noticed me. I was always introduced about five times because I made no impression. I think I'm probably better looking now because I've learned to make the best of the good points and hide the bad ones.

As to those good and bad points, the good ones are obvious (and endless), but the *bad* ones? Well, according to the one person in her professional life who knew her figure best, Edith Head, Grace was: "A little too short-waisted and long-legged, and having a waist that was much too small." She herself was none too fond of her chin and big jaw, preferring to be photographed on her left side.

The message from Grace is clear here: get to know your best and worst features, and make the most (and least) of them, respectively. More importantly, though: remember, it's what's inside that counts. Being beautiful did not matter to Grace—except for being beautiful on the inside, that is. Her stunning good looks may have gotten her started on the ladder to that Hollywood career and her glittering role as a princess, but it was her good manners, kindness, and warmth that made her reach the top. Students of Grace: take note!

chapter six

Royal Romance

"I don't want to be worshipped, I want to be loved."

TRACY LORD, *HIGH SOCIETY*

THE HEADLINES RAINED DOWN like confetti the first week of January 1956. "PRINCE OF MONACO WINS GRACE" said the *St. Petersburg Times*. "GRACE KELLY, PRINCE, PLAN WEDDING," stated the *Ludington Daily News*, before adding, "Hollywood has never been more flabbergasted." But in the grand scheme of flabbergasted, Hollywood paled into insignificance compared to that of Grace Kelly's friends and family when, around December 18, 1955, she called them to announce her engagement.

Not because she was engaged per se. Rather, it was her fiancé du jour who raised eyebrows and dropped jaws. No, it was not French actor Jean-Pierre Aumont, nor yet reconciliation with her old beau Oleg Cassini, she intriguingly relayed. Rather, she doubtless gleefully (knowing Grace's fondness for mischief) divulged to her amazed nearest and dearest, she was engaged to "Europe's most eligible bachelor" Rainier III, Prince of Monaco. Yes, she'd met him only once at the Cannes film festival earlier that year. Yes, she had an engagement ring (a real dazzler from Cartier eventually to be upgraded), and yes, Jack Kelly had given his blessing. A trio of "yes" that form just part of one of the most legendary proposals of marriage, and indeed marriages, ever.

AN EMBARRASSMENT OF SUITORS

She was beautiful, she was charming, and she was available (at least before December 1955). No wonder men had been falling at Grace Patricia Kelly's feet since she'd taken her first elegant steps into womanhood, even popping the question, according to Margaret Kelly: "Men began proposing to my daughter Grace when she was barely fifteen," she once boasted. But before we look at the last impossible-to-resist proposal Grace received, let's see if we can identify three further men who also tried to persuade Grace to dial M for Marriage. From the clues below, and using all your GK know-how, can you pinpoint who they are?

1. Rainier was not the first royal to propose to Grace. As early as 1949 she had enjoyed six dates in New York with a certain king looking for a queen—his second one in fact. This mystery man not only asked for Grace's hand in marriage but also lavished her with jewels, including a gold birdcage housing a diamond-and-sapphire bird. Grace ac-

cepted the jewels though not the proposal, eventually gifting the treasure trove of sparklers to her bridesmaids on the eve of her wedding.

2. Shortly after filming one of the two movies they made together, an old-time Hollywood crooner popped the question, declaring himself "daffy" over Grace. But who was he?

3. Grace enjoyed a romance with this Frenchman on the Riviera and was spotted wining and dining with him in Paris. There was no official proposal but the pair were said to be about to spend the rest of their lives together. Clue: it's not Oleg Cassini.

Answers:

1. Grace's first marriage proposal came from the Shah of Iran, no less. She was aged just twenty when he proposed. Not keen on converting to Islam, she politely declined.

2. Bing Crosby, who was said to be distraught when Grace turned him down.

3. Jean-Pierre Aumont. He would later claim that he totally understood Grace's preference for the Catholic Rainier, citing all the problems their relationship had encountered: "I was Jewish, I had a little girl, I was French."

We'll now take a look at this whirlwind romance, the happy couple's engagement, right through to the so-called wedding of the century and how to plan your own Big Day. Etched in the memories
and minds of millions, Grace's wedding has often been touted as the
ultimate "fairy tale." Not so, according to the woman herself. In fact,
in this chapter we must sadly shake off the fairy dust and break the
supposed romantic spell cast on Rainier and Grace, bringing things
down to earth with a bump as we see what getting wed was *really*
like for Grace.

And if hatching a plan to catch a prince does not chime with you,
fret not; we have plenty more marital morsels besides, when we look
at Grace's many roles as a bride and wife onscreen.

A DECENT PROPOSAL (AT LAST)

Eleven months after filming *To Catch a Thief*, Grace Kelly once again
jetted out to France, this time as part of the US delegation to the
1955 Cannes film festival. In Cannes she bumped into old lover and
friend Jean-Pierre Aumont. The pair fell straight back into each
other's arms and were photographed kissing first in Cannes, then in
Paris. But while M. Aumont was publicly declaring his love for
Grace, she was sending rushed telegrams back to Ma Kelly in Philly
to put a damper on rumors of a torrid affair. But in the public and
Aumont's eyes at least, they were an item, so when, during her visit,
Grace was invited to the Palace of Monaco to meet Prince Rainier
III at the behest of *Paris Match*, it seemed little more than a photo
opportunity. To Grace, was it any more than this? Well, by all ac-
counts she was apathetic about the meeting, if not a little frustrated
due to her tight schedule. And frustration soon rose to irritation

when a power outage in the hotel saw her have to change her outfit *de choix*, which in turn rose to out-and-out anger when the prince was late. Something must have happened that day, though: something about Rainier's manner, about the tour of the palace zoo, where the prince petted a tiger that saw Grace mutter "charming," when asked how she found the prince.

By the autumn of 1955 the ink on the gossip columns still dripped with rumors about Grace and Jean-Pierre Aumont. But Grace wasn't bowled over. *Le pauvre* Jean-Pierre! How could he have known Grace's love life at this point rivaled the complexity of a Hitchcock script? By winter their affair was over, and that vague proposal we've just described was all but forgotten. And in the meantime Grace had penned a brief note to thank the prince for the tour, which started a correspondence that would last throughout filming of *The Swan* and until December.

What happened next is up there in chapter one of The Great Book of Romantic Legends: on the pretext of an annual medical check-up in New York, Prince Rainier dropped by the Kelly family home with his adviser, Father Tucker. Three days of courtship in New York followed. Then, IT happened! The proposal that Grace had been waiting for, from a man she felt she could truly devote her life to. On January 5, 1956, the happy couple's engagement was announced at a small luncheon at the Philadelphia Country Club. At the press conference Grace somewhat disingenuously pooh-poohed the idea she had ever been in love with anyone but her prince, saying she'd only been in love once before with a boy now dead. "I'm very, very happy," continued Grace, wowing the press pack in a stunning champagne-colored silk shirtdress. "I give them my blessing," said Jack Kelly.

Smiles all around on the ground then, but the stars above Hollywood may just have twinkled a little less brilliantly that night amid the fear they were about to lose one of their brightest stars. And how right they were.

THE FINAL CURTAIN

"Before we all knew it, she was gone."

JAMES STEWART

The family blessings bestowed, the arrangements for a grand wedding in Monaco in place, and the world's media well and truly agog . . . but hang on! Wasn't there the small matter of that much fought-over contract with MGM to consider? Short answer, yes. At the time of her engagement Grace was under contract with the film company to make two further movies: *High Society* (1956), of which two months of filming remained, and *Designing Woman* (1957), a romantic comedy set in the world of fashion. Ever the professional, Grace finished the former (and thank goodness for that, it's one of our favorites!) but agreed to a leave of absence from MGM, opening up her role in *Designing Woman* to Lauren Bacall. Another good call from Grace here, ending as she did her Hollywood career with a bang, whereas had she filmed *Designing Woman*, it would have fizzled out with barely a whimper.

THE BURNING QUESTIONS

So she was leaving, it was true, but three questions come to mind that have troubled Grace's biographers and fans ever since.

1. Did Grace *really* think she'd be giving up the movie business?
Friends from that era would say an emphatic "No way!"; the actress Rita Gam argued Grace only realized her career was over as she set sail for her honeymoon. Which just goes to show what friends know, because as early as March 1956, a month before their wedding, Grace and Rainier had been the cover boy and girl for *Paris Match*, with the splash line from Grace: "Je renonce au cinéma" (I'm giving up the movies). "I'm not going back," she went on inside the magazine. "Everything the prince wants suits me, and I respect his judgment." So, in early 1956, instead of learning lines as she had grown accustomed, Grace was studying French, knitting, and brushing up on a much-needed new skill: palace protocol. Grace meant business.

2. It was true, she was bidding adieu to Hollywood—but why?
Grace's star was high, supernova high; her talent acknowledged (Oscar-worthy, in fact); and she and MGM were finally singing more from the same hymn sheet when it came to her choice of roles. Could it really be the matter of love and a wedding that saw her bring down the final curtain on her acting career? This quote from the horse's mouth would imply not: "I'm still pretty young so my makeup call is at 7:30. But I get there and there's Merle Oberon who's been in the chair since five, there's Irene Dunne who's been in the chair since 3:30. They're getting old. Each year my makeup call is a little earlier. And when I look at the other ladies who've been there since dawn, [I think] do I want to live like that? Get me out." Or put more simply: "I loved working at my craft. I didn't particularly like being a movie star," Grace would later tell ABC reporter Pierre Salinger in a 1982 interview.

3. OK, we've now got an idea of why she left—but why so fast?

It's amazing to think, but let's remind ourselves Grace had met Prince Rainier just once before he flew to the States to propose. The timing and speed of his proposal and the subsequent wedding remains a mystery. Even her sister Lizanne would later say, "I don't know why she chose to marry him so quickly." We can speculate as to why, of course: to impress her father perhaps, Grace may have been keen to start a family, or for the professional reasons mentioned above, but we can never truly know. Meanwhile, Rainier's motivations were much more cut and dried: he had no heir and he was the wrong side of thirty. If he were to die without one his principality would have reverted to French rule and its 20,000 citizens would be forced to pay taxes. Monaco was in financial ruin and there was the small matter of a $2 million dowry paid to Monaco by Jack Kelly (some say, with the help of his daughter Grace).

---

*D*o you believe in love at first sight? Of course it's possible that Grace and Rainier were lucky enough to experience this most thrilling, and elusive, of sensations, which was the catalyst for her fleeing Hollywood without a glance back, and so suddenly, too. Now we're going to do something cruel to those of you of a romantic disposition, so if you don't want to know the horrible truth, then it's probably best to scurry back to your turret and hide under the four-poster bed. Because, in actual fact, rather than effusing about their courtship in sentimental gushes, the pair both spoke of it in somewhat dry terms.

The butterflies, the ardor, the passion of that much-dreamed-about state of love at first sight? Well, they're a rarity. And if there's a gargantuan Grace Kelly life lesson to be learned from all of this, it's that when it comes to selecting a husband, counterintuitive as this may sound, it may be best to use your head, not your heart—just as Grace did.

BOWING OUT "GRACE"FULLY

There's another useful life lesson that springs from Grace bidding an end to her Hollywood career: it's knowing when to bow out. And when you do, doing it, well, gracefully and with aplomb. Remember, it's not about doing whatever your man says and kowtowing to male authority. Come on, this is *Grace* we're talking about! Grace who stood up to domineering Jack Kelly (over her move to New York, the acting career, and even the dowry and marriage to Rainier); Grace who had stood up to iron-fisted Dore Schary, MGM's studio head. It's not a symptom of the fan-girl in us if we say quite firmly Grace would not have given up Hollywood for Rainier, if not for the fact she was listening to the person whose counsel she relied on most: her own. So, if like Grace you are feeling flighty, be it toward your career or perhaps a loved one, or if you just have a more general itch you need to scratch, follow these timeless tips before making like a flea-ridden monkey and scratching all over.

BASIC INSTINCT

If an opportunity has appeared on the horizon, use your instinct. It might be big, it could be scary, but sometimes all the advice and good counsel in the world won't tell you what you need to know, while an inner voice niggling at you will. Grace, in her interview with *Vogue* magazine in 1972, admitted instinct played a key part in her decision to marry so quickly: "I didn't really think about it because I act more on instinct and on feeling. I don't sit and ponder. I've discovered that certain truths come all of a sudden." We'd wager that same emotion was at play when she said no to filming *Designing Woman*, instead taking that leave of absence from MGM.

CLIMB EVERY MOUNTAIN

So, you're at the top of your game but something is telling you to try something new. Believe it or not, giving up what you've worked so hard for is not such a bad idea. We're living longer than ever, making the possibilities to change careers never-ending; the number of so-called silver start-ups in business attests to that. So whatever your dream, don't let age or circumstances stop you, and as the song goes, climb every mountain and ford every stream. In short, have a go at whatever life throws at you, and only then will you find your dream.

ONE THING AT A TIME

Having said all this, sometimes in life we have to compromise. Grace wanted to be a Hollywood star, but she wanted to be a wife and mother more. Back in 1954, when baby sister Lizanne had a baby, Grace was clucky. If, to become a mother, she had to turn her back on those fought-over roles and accolades, pragmatic Grace was of the opinion, so be it. So, if you feel overwhelmed by the possibilities life offers, let one aspect of your life take a backseat while you forge ahead with another. Take a leaf out of Grace's (adventure) book and dive into your next schemes and plans, even if it means giving up something else.

THE WEDDING OF THE CENTURY

The next few months in the script of Grace's life would not make much of a movie: matters revolved around practicalities, negotiations, and organization. Grace was, according to Rita Gam: "A quiet eye in the middle of a tremendous hurricane." There was her royal trousseau to put together (aided by a gift of certain of her dresses from MGM), good-byes to be said, negotiations to get out of that MGM contract, and oh, a wedding to arrange. In fact, the latter two went hand in hand. It must have helped Grace along in getting that sabbatical from MGM that she agreed they could film a documentary of her wedding day, titled *Wedding in Monaco*. And this is how Helen Rose, MGM's head costume designer, came to design Grace's wedding gown and their hairdresser fixed her "do" for the Big Day. Rainier, too, would benefit: in filming the event for the whole world to see, his beloved Monaco would get the advertising he felt it needed. It was a win-win for Grace and Rainier, and provided them with a motion picture of their very own in recording their wedding for posterity.

HOW TO PLAN YOUR OWN DREAM WEDDING

Grace and Rainier's wedding was a fabulous spectacle—the numbers involved alone attest to this: 30 million viewers worldwide watched the event on TV; 600 guests attended the religious ceremony on April 19, 1956; 3,000 Monégasques were invited to the function after the civil ceremony; and let's not forget Grace's wedding gown, which had been made with 25 yards of silk taffeta and 100 yards of silk net. All of which, put together in a magnificent wedding cake–shaped bundle, made what commentators at the time called "The Wedding of the Century."

Fancy your own wedding of the century? Need some advice on getting hitched? Well, even if your coffers don't run as deep as those of the Grimaldi or Kelly family, there's much we can learn from lifting the veil on Grace's own Big Day. Let's now take a look at its successes and its failures, and what you can borrow from it, as the poem goes, along with the traditional something old and new, to plan your own special day.

VENUE

When the papers first announced the engagement in early January 1956, the consensus was that the wedding would be in New York or the Kelly family hometown, Philadelphia. By mid-January there was a different news story: Grace Kelly would be marrying in Monaco, at a Catholic Mass at the St. Nicholas Cathedral. As it turned out, there were to be two ceremonies. The first, a civil ceremony, was held on April 18, 1956, in the damask royal throne room at the palace in Monaco, a ceremony required to take place under Monégasque law. The *Washington Post* reported that day that it was a "kissless marriage" characterized by a "tense sadness." This, the *WP* reporter explained, was because of the nervous collapse of one of the prince's aides before the event. But it's also true that Rainier had warned Grace she should expect a lack of emotion at her wedding. (Little could she have known, this would set the tone for the entire marriage.) The following day's event at the intimidatingly huge St.

Nicholas Cathedral was equally serious: Grace followed her husband-to-be's advice. She was the very picture of serenity as she wed him to become Her Serene Highness, Princess Grace of Monaco.

WEDDING WORDS OF WISDOM

The best-laid plans of mice and men often go awry, said Robert Burns, and weddings are no exception. Be it the illness of one of your guests, a problem with the food or flowers, or inappropriate language or behavior from your future in-laws, you'd be well advised to take any hiccups in your stride. Grace was never a diva and certainly not on her wedding day. As to the venue, if you wish to marry in an intimate setting but friends and relatives are on your case for a swankier do, take a leaf out of Grace's wedding planner and get married twice. Two outfits, two cakes, double the fun!

TRADITIONS

In 1956, when Grace spoke to *Paris Match*, she confirmed that she wouldn't be showing the prince her sumptuous Helen Rose gown until the day of the wedding because she wanted to keep it a surprise for him. It's a pity Rainier did the same for Grace. His military-looking costume of black and gold, which he had designed himself, could easily have upstaged the bride. One tradition she did not want to stick to, however, was separate rooms on the night before the wedding. Even though they were already legally married before the church service on April 19, Rainier and Grace spent the previous night apart: "This is absolutely Victorian!" said Grace, but she went along with Rainier's wishes, a theme that was to define their marriage for years to come.

WEDDING WORDS OF WISDOM

Keep with tradition and don't show your husband your dress . . . or what's underneath it until your wedding day.

THE BRIDAL PARTY

Grace chose six of her closest New York friends as her bridesmaids and her sister Peggy was a witness on the day of the civil ceremony. The whole Kelly clan were present, save younger sister Lizanne, who was expecting (and would later call her baby girl Grace). On the day of the religious ceremony, Grace's father, Jack Kelly, dispensed with tradition and held Grace's arm until Rainier had entered the church. For once he was right by her side and did not leave her stranded.

WEDDING WORDS OF WISDOM

Don't hold back! If ever there was a time when you deserve an entourage, this is it. Abide by etiquette by all means, choosing flower girls from the groom's or your side of the family, but otherwise this is the time to let your closest friends be there for you. But do be sensitive to your desired bridesmaids' feelings: think twice if someone in your circle is always the bridesmaid and never the bride. She may not want to be an integral part of your big day.

FLOWERS

Roses had always been personal favorites of the bride's and would be significant throughout her life . . . and after her death. It was with an enormous bouquet of roses that Oleg Cassini originally captured Grace's heart. And when she died in 1982, a rose garden was named after her, containing 4,000 rose bushes on the slope of Monaco's Fontvieille Park. Small wonder then that her matrons of honor on her wedding day carried bouquets of tea roses. The bride herself held lily of the valley and her Juliet cap contained orange blossom, while the young flower girls carried white daisies. Later, she would pen a much-loved work on flower arranging, *My Book of Flowers*.

WEDDING WORDS OF WISDOM

The devil is in the detail. For example, the delicate pink of the tea roses carried by Grace's bridesmaids are a nod to the damask pink she wore the previous day at the civil ceremony. Remember, the photos of your wedding day are captured for posterity and it's well worth paying attention to the small things.

THE GUESTS

Of the 600 wedding guests it is interesting to note just how few of Grace's fellow film stars were there. David Niven, yes, and Cary Grant, her good friend Ava Gardner, too. But notable by his absence was her beloved director, Sir Alfred Hitchcock, and Frank Sinatra excused himself for fear of upstaging the bride. As to the world's shakers and movers, Jackie Kennedy and Aristotle Onassis came, as did the Aga Khan, but the British royals, for instance, were said to find the whole affair decidedly distasteful and sent a minor emissary.

WEDDING WORDS OF WISDOM

Choose who you wish to attend, not for show, not for favors but because you genuinely wish them to bless your betrothal. And if anyone's conspicuous by their absence, do what Grace did: throw the biggest wedding you could ever imagine and no one will ever notice. Besides, rather an absent friend than a glum guest as German playwright Friedrich Schiller notes in this apt quotation: "A gloomy guest fits not a wedding feast."

THE FAIRY-TALE WEDDING

"I don't want my wedding spoiled by intruders."

TRACY SAMANTHA LORD, *HIGH SOCIETY*

So, you want the fairy-tale wedding: the whirlwind romance, the knight on a white charger, the masses swooning on your every word and move? That's all well and good but remember those Disney movies only show what happens up to the point where you meet the prince. Grace herself was extremely pragmatic on the matter: "The idea of my life as a fairy tale is itself a fairy tale" she is often quoted as saying. What's more, you might plan an enormous everything-a-princess-could-wish-for kind of affair only to discover that you wish, as Grace and Rainier did, that you'd run off to a wedding chapel in the hills. She later told a magazine that she only enjoyed the private moments of her big day, while her daughter Caroline told Barbara Walters: "My parents hated their wedding. They didn't even look at pictures of it for a year."

WEDDING WORDS OF WISDOM

As someone wise once said: "Weddings are nice but marriages are even nicer." You may dream of the fairy-tale wedding only to quickly drift into a horror show of a marriage. By all means rush in as Grace did, but only do so if you trust your instincts. Marriage is hard work and in the chapters to come we'll see how Grace learned this the hard way. But for now, let's leave her setting sail from the shores of Monaco for a six-week honeymoon sailing the Mediterranean as she waves good-bye to the crowds of adoring Monégasques who had warmly welcomed their new princess.

MARRIED-IN-THE-MOVIES

It's telling of the roles meted out to women in Hollywood during the early 1950s how often Grace played the part of somebody's wife or prospective wife, or girlfriend, rather than just someone in her own right. Even in one of her most cherished roles as Lisa Fremont in *Rear Window*, Grace's contribution is often belittled as "Jimmy Stewart's girlfriend." Small wonder she often cursed that she did not want to be "used as scenery" in her movies and seized the chance to play Georgie in *The Country Girl*.

The problem is that Grace plays the part of the wife and girlfriend so well, it seems only natural that men would be falling at her feet. And whether a wife tempted by a torrid affair, a girlfriend trying to woo her commitment-phobic boyfriend, or a society gal with men falling at her feet, Grace's charms on celluloid are enviable. Want some of that to rub off on you? Feel like capturing the heart of a particular someone, or bringing a straying husband back in line? Take a cue from the following scenarios to find out what the fictional Grace would do in all matters betrothal and bridal and how to cope with marriage on the Big Day and beyond.

14 Hours

A very small role in this, Grace's first movie, is nevertheless notable for the fact that it sees her character, Louise Fuller, having second thoughts about a divorce (she eventually decides against signing her divorce papers). This is the first of many a parallel with Grace's own life. Divorce was never in question, but those harder times in the palace may have had Grace taking comfort from her rosary beads and trying to come to terms with the fact that marriage is, above all, a contract. And contracts mean hard work! Truth be told, the workaday element of marriage wasn't much of a struggle for Grace, though. Remember her hard work throughout her life: the acting and elocution lessons, the countless TV roles? Her tenacity and strong work ethic applied to her marriage as well. Like Louise Fuller, divorce for Grace would not be the answer to marital strife.

A MARRIED-IN-THE-MOVIES TIP: Take a cue from Grace's character here. If you're navigating the choppy waters of a difficult relationship, sometimes it pays to look at the bigger picture. As Grace herself said of her real-life marriage: "There are stormy periods in every marriage. They call for a lot of humility and the willingness to be wrong—even if you're not!"

High Noon

In her first main role Grace plays Amy Kane, the Quaker pacifist wife of the town of Hadleyville's marshal. The action for this much-lauded Western begins at the wedding of Gary Cooper's Will Kane to the very pretty, bonnet-headed Amy; the townsfolk are all there to see the wedding and watch Will, who is handing in his badge, to settle down with Amy and lead the life of a shopkeeper. Step up the Miller gang, seeking to avenge their brother Frank Miller, whom Will has turned over to the county sheriff. What follows is a waiting game for Frank, just released from jail and set to arrive on the noon train, with a climax that sees Amy Kane going against her religious beliefs for the love of her man.

In a line that spookily anticipates her nerves at the crowds on her own wedding day, as she steps out of the small registrar office Grace's Amy Kane says: "People ought to be alone when they get married." We wonder if this line echoed through Grace's head as she climbed the steps to St. Nicholas Cathedral with the entire world watching on April 19, 1956.

A MARRIED-IN-THE-MOVIES TIP: Grace's role may not have stretched her acting ability or her endurance in *High Noon* (she is not on screen that much), but hers is a pivotal role and imparts the message of the movie and also of her marriage: stand by your man, no matter what.

The Country Girl

Grace's role in this dramatic 1954 version of an earlier Broadway play can be summed up in one line stated by her protagonist, Georgie Elgin, midway through the movie: "I'm a drunkard's wife." Not just any old drunkard, mind you. Her husband, Frank (played by Bing Crosby), is an ex-theater star, his career blighted by booze and the memory of a horrific family accident; he is then hired for a new show by director Bernie Dodd (William Holden), albeit for dubious reasons. Bernie and Georgie lock horns over Frank's drinking (Bernie does not believe he's a drunk), and later, after much heated argument, they lock lips.

It was not only a departure for Grace but also for Bing Crosby, who'd previously crooned and swooned his way through many a romantic lead. But it works. Both excel and we need several buckets of ice water to cool down after the tense romantic scenes between Grace and William Holden.

A MARRIED-IN-THE-MOVIES TIP: The movie was billed as a hard-hitting drama but its tagline "How far should a woman go to redeem the man she loves?" hints that it's also a film with deep-seated romantic notions. When Georgie walks off, not into the sunset but onto a dark and slightly ominous street to reclaim her man, the idea of sticking together through thick and thin is cemented; this is an endorsement for the state of marriage, make no mistake, even if the execution is slightly bleak. When William Holden's Bernie says of Grace's Georgie: "I never knew there was such a woman, so loyal and steadfast," one thinks of Rainier, later in the palace, when things had gotten difficult between himself and Grace. In Grace, Rainier had found his Georgie.

The Swan

Jay Kanter, her agent, recalled that Grace was very anxious to land the part of Princess Alexandra in *The Swan*, and finally Dore Schary of MGM agreed it was perfect for her. We can see the appeal of this script to Grace. Not only had she already played the role in a TV version in the early fifties, but it had also been a hit on Broadway in the 1920s, so had the theatrical element she adored. Grace's film version enjoys the intimate feeling of a play, being set mainly in one location (a palace) and with few characters, all enjoying some great lines. But some of Grace's biographers sell her short in this part. What a shame! We'd wager she plays her first (and only) headlining role brilliantly, delivering with perfect comic timing some very funny lines. As a comedy of manners about the desperation of the aristocracy to continue its lineage, it is both funny and convincing, and as a romance both sweet and sour. In short, as a swan song for Grace's Hollywood career, it is perfect.

Grace plays Alexandra, a young princess whose family have been dethroned during the Napoleonic era. Her mother is desperate to marry her off to the Crown Prince Albert (Alec Guinness), but when he arrives at the palace he is less than Prince Charming and takes every opportunity to make Alexandra and her mother, Beatrix, feel uncomfortable. Alexandra's feelings for the young and handsome tutor Dr. Nicholas Agi become simultaneously warmer as the prince's charms grow ever colder, helped along by a spot of matchmaking by her mother. Only the arrival of his mother, Queen Maria Dominika, causes Albert to finally melt and admit his true feelings for Alexandra.

The parallels with Grace's own life are somewhat spooky. A reluctant and recalcitrant prince who has "turned down every princess in Europe" chooses Grace for his bride, while Grace's character in, perhaps, a nod and a wink to her reputation is said to resemble a distant relative in a portrait in the palace: Elena the Ice Queen. At the time of filming Grace had already met Rainier and was receiving letters almost daily from him, a fact that she hotly denied. And yet Alexandra, like Grace, gets her prince by the movie's climax. "I always said dear Alexandra would have her opportunity in the end," states her great-aunt at the beginning.

And how true, for despite Grace's many lovers they were simply dress rehearsals for her natural role as a princess-to-be. A role for which Grace's film mother says she should be "gracious and dignified, warm and charming and amusing." Small wonder Rainier on that meeting, and on his search for a wife, should pick up on those same characteristics in Grace.

A MARRIED-IN-THE-MOVIES TIP: First impressions can be wrong. You may meet your very own handsome young Dr. Agi, but sometimes duty (including duty to yourself) should take precedence over desire. Remember what Grace said about being able to love many men? It's true, but in her case it was not the big love affair that led to marriage; she made a conscious decision to go for the dependable. OK, so Rainier *was* a prince, but it was hardly *the* romance of the century! In a nutshell, sometimes your best match might just be made here on earth, rather than in heaven—and do you know what? That's perfectly OK!

chapter seven

Princess Grace

"She made as good a princess as she was an actress."

JAMES STEWART

I N MODERN PARLANCE THE word "princess" often conjures up thoughts of the Disney version: of romance and recalcitrance, petticoats and pink. Or else the word is used as shorthand to describe a spoiled brat, the arrogant young woman who is prone to a temper tantrum or three. Her Serene Highness Princess Grace of Monaco was neither of these models of princess. Rather, she took her position very seriously, endowed it with her usual charm and elegance, and worked hard at the role.

In fact, so hard did she work that those white gloves may just have gotten a little shabby: for the Monégasque people, she worked hard in bringing culture, tourism, and the arts to Monaco, in a huge boost for the country's ailing economy; for her husband she worked hard for all those reasons, but also in updating certain outdated protocols within the Palace of Monaco; and she worked hard for her charities, La Leche League and the Red Cross among others. In short, as she had done throughout her movie career, Grace put her heart and soul into the job of princess and helped give new meaning to the word.

Yet all was not rosy in the gardens (or elsewhere) in the Palace of Monaco. Adjusting to life in her new home did not come easy for Grace. As an American, certain European traditions threw her (her favorite food was hamburger for one, so that was always going to be tough!), and the gap left by family and friends in the United States turned out to be a gaping one. More problematic still, the relationship with Rainier was troubled from the starting blocks. But Grace played her "last role" as a real-life princess to a T, eventually winning the hearts and minds of the Monégasque people and even impressing the most difficult of folk: namely the Kelly family back home.

We'll now take a look at all these aspects of Grace's second life in Monaco: at her relationship with Rainier, how she stayed well connected to the great and good back home, and in so doing how she brought a touch of Hollywood glamour to Monte Carlo. We'll also contemplate what made Grace's personality so suited to the title of princess and how you can emulate this to become a princess of your very own. And we don't mean by playing the princess in a pejorative sense; rather we mean by putting all your efforts into whatever life throws at you, even if that just so happens to be the title Her Serene Highness.

WHAT'S IN A NAME?

It's worth noting how the word "princess" has become so overused in the modern age that its original and truest definition as the daughter of a monarch or wife of a prince has almost been forgotten. But could you, if pushed, identify a real princess from a fake? Oh, you think so, do you? Well, take a look at the list below and see if you can tick off the bona fide princesses. Unfortunately we don't have any peas or feathered mattresses at our disposal to help with this task, so you'll have to make do with the more mundane method of using your little gray cells:

Princess Tiana	Princess Leia
Princess Haya	Princess Letizia
Princess Tiammi	Princess Alexandra

Answer:

In fact, only two of these women are real-life princesses: Letizia, Princess of Asturias, who is wife of Felipe, Prince of Asturias and heir-apparent to the Spanish throne, and Princess Haya of Jordan, one of the King of Jordan's daughters. Princess Tiammi, we're afraid, is anything but, being the daughter of glamour model Katie Price aka Jordan and her ex-partner Peter Andre. Tiana is the latest Disney princess from *The Princess and the Frog*. And if you don't know your Princess Alexandra from your Princess Leia in the movies, then it's back to beginners' lessons in Grace Kelly for you!

PUTTING MONACO ON THE MAP

"I became a princess before I had time to imagine what it would be."

GRACE PATRICIA KELLY

We last saw Grace only just crowned a princess, sailing the Med on her honeymoon with her new husband. There's no denying romance flourished during that honeymoon (the birth of Princess Caroline nine months and four days after the holiday attests to this), but not everything went according to plan. Grace caught a cold on the first day and while Rainier immediately got his sea legs, much to her chagrin Grace discovered that she was a landlubber. More worrying still, as she lay prone in her cabin, came the slow realization that her Hollywood career might truly be at an end.

So, was the honeymoon over, in fact, before the royals' honeymoon was even over?

Things did not improve upon arrival at the Palace of Monaco, where Grace discovered a chill wind blew through its corridors rather than a soft Mediterranean breeze: the palace staff and Rainier's family displayed a decidedly icy comportment toward the so-called ice queen. What's more, there was an avalanche of protocol to overcome, and just imagine the fiercely independent Grace's dismay when she discovered her husband was overprotective: "He has me cornered," she told a friend in the 1960s. "I can't move, I can't go anywhere—I have no freedom."

It was not the fairy-tale ending after the fairy-tale wedding. But in this time of adversity, what did Grace do? Did she run back to Hollywood, tail between her legs? No, she did what any intelligent free spirit would do and made the best of her circumstances. Though homesick, she kept up with the United States through TV and newspapers, she visited old friends and family, and she also started a family of her own. Then, in a coup de grâce counteracting the bad feeling toward her from the Monégasque people, she helped Rainier with his plan to transform Monaco from an ailing principality into a glamorous Riviera holiday destination. Indeed, by the mid-1960s even her Hollywood friends were coming to visit in droves, perhaps a small case of the mountain coming to Mohammad. Clever Grace!

---

*H*ere's an example of how you, similarly to she who we adore, can embrace whatever life throws at you and do something altogether surprisingly splendid. In Grace's case, she used her wit, warmth, and powers of persuasion to help make the Principality of Monaco *the* destination for the rich and famous. Or, as Grace's former fiancé, Oleg Cassini, put it: "Grace made a sinking boat beautiful again. She attracted people—the cult of Grace Kelly. They were coming to Monaco like Arabs come to Mecca. It was a pilgrimage of the affluent to Monaco. Grace grabbed all the successful people to come and everybody wanted to be there. This was *the* spot. She did it."

How about you? Do you have a Monaco moment in you? Could you tap into an area of unfulfilled potential in your life? Or do you have a friend, a lover, or a child requiring a much-needed boost, who could make use of your time and expertise or your contacts? The secret here is to have a vision, or to share somebody else's, and to take time and energy to bring this to fruition. Just like Monaco was for Grace and Rainier. And there you go—

that metaphorical piece of cut glass you've suffered angst over could become a showstopping diamond.

A TIGHT SPOT

It was not only matters economical that were aided by a large sprinkling of Grace's stardust over Monaco, but matters political, too. The first few years of Grace's reign as princess in the early 1960s had brought not only tourism to the principality, but with its tax haven status, Monaco also attracted many businesses: British, American, German, and French. The latter irked France's President de Gaulle, who considered annexing the principality, and when Rainier banned trading of Radio Monaco on the French stock exchange, de Gaulle threw down the gauntlet: unless Monaco's citizens and its businesses paid taxes to Paris, its sovereignty and independence were threatened.

While Rainier worked hard on the front line to improve relations with France, Her Serene Highness also played a key role. As the ante was upped and there was talk of Monaco being "enclosed in barbed wire" as Grace put it, she used her star status to interest the world's media in the affair and applied all her charm and those excellent negotiating skills (remember that MGM contract?) to win over de Gaulle. In 1962 a new treaty constitution was signed in Monaco, de Gaulle relented, and disaster was averted.

HOW TO BE A PRINCESS

"Kind hearts are more than coronets."

FROM ALFRED, LORD TENNYSON'S 1842 POEM "LADY CLARA VERE DE VERE"

We've already established that Grace's life as a princess was built around hard work, not daydreams or an easy-won life of luxury. Though not a fan of such things, she attended many social functions: balls, dinners, and parties, but she also toiled tirelessly for her chosen charities and putting her all into raising a family. Here then was a princess who paid as much heed to conscientiousness and courtliness as to the glitz and glamour of being a royal. Not only this, but she carried out her role with characteristic good grace and exquisite manners.

She was a princess in the broadest sense of the word, without any of the pejorative meaning it has taken on in modern life. Want to be a bona fide princess like Grace? Remember, it's not the tiara that makes the princess: it's strength of character, hard work, and good manners. And if you want to know more, herewith our mini guide with a few practical princess pointers along the way—pink, glass slippers, and tantrums not required.

WORK IT!

First and foremost, Grace's success as a princess was founded on pure, unadulterated hard work. Her schedule did not revolve around sleeping in and being pampered: she was up at 8 a.m.; then after breakfast she would fulfill her duties in the palace, planning events up to six months in advance, in such demand was she. After lunch she would spend some time with the children and always read them a bedtime story. On top of this, Grace acted as an ambassador for Monaco and her chosen charities and was a philanthropist to boot. No wonder she was often coming down with a cold!

PRACTICAL PRINCESS POINTER: Want to succeed at a new challenge? Well, to channel our amazing Grace, you'll have to slog your way to be successful at it. And if there's an about-face in your life—you move abroad perhaps, or have a complete career overhaul—you'll need to plan and work hard to adapt to your new role. Once there, be professional. As Grace herself said about her role as a princess: "I'd like to think I'm a professional at my job, no matter what it may be."

THOROUGHLY MODERN MANNERS

Grace attended Ravenhill convent school from the age of four until she'd completed the eighth grade (around thirteen-and-a-half). It was here that she learned to wear a hat and white gloves. And of course nothing says decorum more than a nun. The Stevens School in Germantown, PA, where Grace spent her teenage years, was the closest the United States would come to a finishing school, being a school for "young ladies." Grace learned how to pour a cup of tea and other matters of etiquette. It might not have taught her the basics of math (an area in which she did not excel) but it did teach her the manners and mores that stood her in good stead throughout her career, hailed as she was for being refined and of good breeding.

PRACTICAL PRINCESS POINTER: Minding your p's and q's will give you more chance of zooming through the alphabet to "S" for "Success." In a world where please and thank you seem to belong to a bygone era, it doesn't take much to stand out from the crowd and be remembered for a kind and polite word here and there.

> *"Manners are an agent for positive engagement,*
> *and for getting more out of people."*
>
> DEBRETT'S ETIQUETTE FOR GIRLS

SHOW YOUR BEST SIDE

So far in our story of Grace we've only lightly touched on one of the factors that made her such an exceptional human being—that is, her naturally warm and effervescent personality. She may have been hailed as an ice queen early on, but in real life Grace was far from it: she was funny, warm, and good spirited, as these personal accounts attest to:

> *"She was such a happy, funny person."*
>
> PRINCESS CAROLINE

> *"She wasn't stuffy. She had a mischievous sense of humor, a glint of naughtiness in her eye, and a great passion for limericks—even saucy ones."*
>
> LOUISETTE LEVY-SOUSSAN AZZOAGLIO, GRACE'S PA FOR NINETEEN YEARS

Grace herself did not wish to be remembered for her stardom, her status, or her stunning good looks. In fact, when interviewed by

Pierre Salinger in 1982, it was her character she mentioned. "I'd like to be remembered as a decent human being and a caring one," she said. We're sure if we put a pea under her bed the night after this interview, Grace would have woken up black and blue, for there speaks a true princess!

PRACTICAL PRINCESS POINTER: Of course you can't change your personality, but learn from Grace here. Behave nicely in the playground of life and good things will come your way. The reverse, I'm afraid, you less than well-mannered misses, is also true. And just remember being a princess is about attitude as much as status. As Celeste Holm, Grace's co-star in *High Society*, said of her: "As far as I was concerned, she was a princess long before she married."

BELIEVE IN YOURSELF . . . BUT ONLY SO FAR

In later life, Grace came to take herself and her role as Her Serene Highness very seriously . . . *too* seriously, some might say. She came close to living up to her "Ice Queen" tag later in the 1970s and there are examples of her appearing distant and unwelcoming, even rude. *So* not like Grace! But, as we'll discover in a moment, the early seventies were her unhappiest years, and so her change of mood, as she also endured the "change of life," is perhaps hardly surprising.

PRACTICAL PRINCESS POINTER: Don't do things halfheartedly: believing in them will make difficult times more palatable. However, you can also learn from Grace's uncharacteristic mistake here: don't take yourself too seriously, remain true to yourself, and have the strength of character not to believe your own hype.

TIMES OF TROUBLE

If the road to her prince had been somewhat bumpy, with Grace stopping off to admire many a male view along the way, the marriage itself was ridden with potholes—and, if the rumors are to be believed, lovers. In fact, as early as 1957, rumors sprang up that not everything in the new house of Grimaldi was a bed of Grace's beloved roses. So soon? you might think. Well, yes. And as you shake your head in sympathy with Grace, you may do so a little more vigorously when we reveal that just three months into her marriage Grace heard that Rainier was keeping a mistress. "I know he has affairs with other women," she later told a friend. "That's very frustrating to me, and it makes me very, very unhappy." Now here's where Grace did not have one of her proudest moments: when she retaliated in kind, rekindling romances, or so it's said, with Marlon Brando, Frank Sinatra, and David Niven, among others.

But fidelity was not the couple's only problem. Early on, they discovered that their tastes were very different—a traditional list of "his and hers" preferences, if you will. Creative, imaginative Grace loved the arts, the ballet, her beloved theater, poetry, and books; macho Rainier, meanwhile, was a man's man, who loved sports and politics and the company of other men. The early years were also hard for practical reasons. In a moment of rare public disclosure, Rainier would later admit to his biographer Peter Hawkins that he knew it had been tough for Grace in adjusting to palace rules and protocol, but that she had "this ability to put on a mask when necessary. It's all to do with her studies in dramatic art."

By the 1970s the couple were living apart, ostensibly because Grace had to chaperone Caroline at school in Paris, but as she told a friend: "It was our way of being separated." So there was Grace enchanting Paris with her presence, enjoying all the cultural delights offered by the city, and being linked to several young men, who she mischievously called her "toy boys." And there was Rainier, playing the bachelor, cavorting in nightclubs with the international jet set.

And yet the pair—perhaps out of duty, perhaps for their children, or maybe even for love—remained married, celebrating their twenty-fifth wedding anniversary at the home of Frank and Barbara Sinatra with family and close friends. Rainier's loving toast to his wife was by all accounts a real tear-jerker: "My life and the lives of so many have never been the same since the day this wonderful woman entered my world," he said. "I adore her more today, more than ever before. She is my princess and I salute her." So, was it the fairy-tale ending to the fairy-tale wedding after all? Perhaps not, but the 1980s did mark, so close friends have said, a new stage in the relationship. How tragic then that this revivification of their romance was cut tragically short by Grace's accident in September 1982.

---

*G*race tutorial alert! If there's a rocky patch in your relationship, be it in a marriage, in a friendship, or with a family member, remember most things can be overcome, and time, as they say, heals many a wound. But don't leave apologies or attempts at reconciliation too long: life can be cruel, and never more so when it is taken away too soon.

SHE SAID WHAT NOW?

Remember your royal radar from earlier on? We hope you managed to identify the true princesses from their plastic counterparts. But can you now pinpoint which princess, real or imagined, said the following words? Time to put your thinking tiaras on and match the quote to the princess.

A. Being a princess isn't all it's cracked up to be.	**1.** Princess Leia Organa of Alderaan
B. I can't be a princess! I'm still waiting for normal body parts to arrive.	**2.** Princess Haya of Jordan
C. I know I'm very lucky…I love being who I am. A lot of it is quite normal.	**3.** Princess Alexandra (*The Swan*)
D. I consider it my inherited duty to help relieve the plight of people who suffer the devastating effects of poverty.	**4.** Diana, Princess of Wales
E. I don't know who you are or where you came from, but from now on you'll do as I tell you, OK?	**5.** Princess Beatrice of York
F. I want to tell you everything that's in my heart.	**6.** Mia Thermopolis (*The Princess Diaries*)

Answers:

A—4: Diana, Princess of Wales, was the queen of a nation's heart and it was this organ she wore on her sleeve when revealing innermost thoughts such as these to the general public in the mid-1990s after her split from Prince Charles.

B—6: Mia Thermopolis from *The Princess Diaries* is just a normal girl when she discovers that she is actually heir-apparent to the throne of Genovia.

C—5: Princess Beatrice of York, fifth in line to the British throne, protests how in touch she is with the common people.

D—2: In saying these heartfelt words Princess Haya of Jordan reveals herself to be a true princess in the manner of a Grace or a Diana.

E—1: Everyone's favorite plucky princess, here is Leia from *Star Wars*—a true royal role model for all aspiring princesses.

F—3: And here's Grace as Princess Alexandra, with words that form a counterpoint to true life at the time of filming of *The Swan*—when she was doing anything but revealing to the world what was truly in her heart.

A TALE OF TWO PRINCESSES

In 1981 a certain wedding out-royaled, out news-storied, and out-shone Grace and Rainier's nuptials twenty-five years earlier. It was July 29 and thousands of Londoners lined the streets to see a shy, blossoming twenty-year-old woman marry the eldest son of Britain's

Queen Elizabeth II in what the press dubbed "The Wedding of the Century." But hold on! Hadn't the royal Monégasque couple owned this honor since their own big day, a quarter of a century previously? Well, yes. But when Lady Diana Spencer became Princess of Wales there are those who would say she also made off with Grace's privileged position as both the world's and the media's favorite princess. Now we don't like to play favorites, but we rather beg to differ. To corroborate this, let's hold a right royal tournament and pit the two princesses against each other to see who can win the most points—or in this case, tiaras—and be crowned the ultimate princess.

THE NUMBERS GAME

Both Grace and the Grimaldi family may have had clout in the international world of the great and good, but they were punching below their weight in comparison to the might of the Windsors and the great British royal family. So, while Grace's wedding boasted 30 million TV viewers in 1956, Charles and Diana's nuptials attracted 750 million worldwide, and while 3,000 Monégasques partied with Grace and Rainier, some 600,000 people lined London's streets in 1981. The Grimaldis, we're afraid to say, were outnumbered. *In the first round of our tournament, it's five tiaras to Diana and a measly three to Grace.*

DIANA: 👑 👑 👑 👑 👑
GRACE: 👑 👑 👑

FAMILY MATTERS

Both women's marriages have oft been touted as being of convenience, manufactured to produce sons and heirs for princes seeking to continue their family lines. Physical examinations carried out on both prior to their weddings attest to the importance of their ability to propagate and the fact that both were pregnant with their firstborns so soon after their honeymoons speaks volumes. We suppose it's just as well that Grace and Diana were such natural mothers and so early on, for their children were beacons of hope through times of trouble and strife. And despite (or perhaps *because* of) marital disharmony each of them was incredibly close to their children. One only has to see how the eyes of William, Harry, Caroline, Albert, and Stephanie light up when they speak of their mothers to know the massive weight carried by their losses. *When it came to motherhood, Grace and Diana were on an even par and we'd like to award each woman . . . trumpet call: four tiaras.*

DIANA: ♛ ♛ ♛ ♛
GRACE: ♛ ♛ ♛ ♛

IN THE PUBLIC EYE

Marrying into royalty was not an easy path for these woman, who had the public spotlight trained on them at full beam from the moment they said "I do" (or in Grace's case, "Je veux"). But here's a key difference in their attitudes. Throughout her marriage, Diana courted publicity, which peaked when she split from Charles and enjoyed that public "Look at Me, World!" Taj Mahal photo opportunity, as well as her TV interview with Martin Bashir. Grace, on the other hand, was the soul of discretion. Even during the 1970s when she lived in Paris with her daughter Caroline, she did her best to dampen down rumors of marital strife by writing to the newspapers and reminding them of their responsibilities. *And so the award for Princess Who Dealt Best with the Press goes to . . . Grace with five tiaras. It's a "look-at-me" three for Diana.*

DIANA: ♕ ♕ ♕
GRACE: ♕ ♕ ♕ ♕ ♕

STYLE PRINCESSES

Another echo in the lives of the two women is their roles as fashion icons. In the 1980s, Diana's every sartorial move was followed with a keen eye by the fashion pack, mirroring Grace's stellar sartorial status back in the 1950s. It's interesting to note, though, that while the 1980s have recently made a comeback, the "Diana look" has been left on the shelf. Looking back, it's almost *too* eighties for the eighties—the puffed sleeves and giant ball gowns, lurid colors and those enormous shoulder pads. Conversely, Grace's fashion stock continues to rise with the timeless elegance of her look and the current love of all things vintage going perfectly hand in white-gloved hand. As to their wedding gowns, we need only consider which princess Catherine Middleton's gown gives a nod to in order to see which dress remains a classic. *Put your white-gloved hands together for a five-tiara win for Grace in this round, and another three for Diana.*

DIANA: ♕ ♕ ♕
GRACE: ♕ ♕ ♕ ♕ ♕

DOING THE RIGHT THING

More meaningfully, both women will be remembered for their charity work: Princess Diana for Centrepoint, National AIDS Trust, and the Diana, Princess of Wales Memorial Fund; Grace for the Princess Grace Memorial Fund, La Leche League, and the Red Cross. Our princesses were no slackers and made genuine good of the world's spotlight being trained on them. *Well done, girls! It's five tiaras each for you.*

DIANA: 👑 👑 👑 👑 👑
GRACE: 👑 👑 👑 👑 👑

ADDING UP THE SCORES

DIANA:	GRACE:
👑👑👑👑	👑👑👑
👑👑👑👑	👑👑👑👑
👑👑👑	👑👑👑👑👑
👑👑👑	👑👑👑👑👑
👑👑👑👑👑	👑👑👑👑👑

We're not surprised to discover that it's Princess Grace who comes out on top. Of course we may be a little biased, but we think it's a fair result. Yes, the lives of the twentieth century's most celebrated princesses enjoy some striking parallels, but to our minds, Grace will always be the number-one real-life princess, carrying off the role as she did with just a tad more je ne sais quoi than the at-times naïve and intellectually less capable Diana.

As an endnote, it's worth mentioning the pair met only twice (the second time being at the wedding of Charles and Diana). The first was only weeks after Diana's engagement when she was not yet accustomed to the constant gaze of the world's media. It was March 1981 at Goldsmiths' Hall in London and an event where Prince Charles was guest of honor and Princess Grace had been invited to give a poetry reading. During an interval, Grace noticed Diana's discomfort in a dress two sizes too small for her and took her off to the ladies' room for a word of advice. Poor Diana! She poured her heart out to Grace and made something of a song and dance over all the press attention she had been getting. "Don't worry, dear," Grace characteristically quipped. "You'll see—it'll only get worse!"

How portentous this now sounds, given the tragic outcome for both these remarkable women. And putting playfulness to one side, we now come to the saddest parallel: their untimely deaths in automobile accidents. Diana died so young, aged thirty-six, just when it seemed her life was coming together; and fifty-three-year-old Grace had also found a new serenity, a new connection with her husband. Their untimely deaths only add to their legendary status.

chapter eight

Family Ties

"I'd like to be remembered in terms of my family."
GRACE PATRICIA KELLY

F AMILY MATTERS, SO THEY say, and it mattered very much to Grace Patricia Kelly. All her life she strove to be an exceptional daughter, sister, wife, and mother—and, for the most part, was rewarded with strong lifelong bonds with all her family. Though her parents were hard to please, expressing misgivings about her career, and later her choice of husband, Grace accepted their many meddlings and allowed them to influence her decision making up to a point. They remained a constant in her life and were frequent visitors to Monaco, along with all three of her siblings, while she herself would often return to her hometown in Philadelphia for family functions long after she was crowned Princess Grace.

Not that the Kelly nor the Grimaldi household was a picture-perfect example of the white-picket-fenced 1950s idyll. Life was not always a slice of Mom's homemade apple pie. There are some who say much of what Grace achieved or *tried* to achieve was to impress her father, the hyper-critical and domineering Jack Kelly. Meanwhile her mother, Margaret, was at times no less of a difficult figure in her life. (Remember *that* article exposing Grace's feelings about her past lovers, and published so close to the wedding?) Amazingly, none of this seemed to matter to conscientious, eager-to-please Grace. Even when times got tough she remained the dutiful daughter and was said to have won Jack Kelly over by the time he reached old age.

Complex, sometimes poignant, we'll now look at Grace's relationship with her parents in more depth and then reveal how you can keep in step with Grace's family values in order to get along better with your own kith and kin. Even more complex was Grace's relationship with her children, who she adored and tried to raise to the very best of her ability—a characteristic worth emulating and one we'll delve deep into here, as, to finish this chapter, we discuss Grace's parenting style.

MR. AND MRS. JACK KELLY

DADDY'S GIRL

Why Grace married Rainier in such a rush; her love of older married men; in later years, our heroine's steadfast commitment to an at-times loveless marriage . . . What, if the reams of paper afforded to the matter are correct, do these three items have in common? If you know the answer, well done—and give yourself a well-deserved pat on the back—but if you don't, then it's back to chapter one and a quick bit of revision about Grace's childhood. It's to that time that we turn to answer this conundrum, and to give some thought to the extraordinary influence Jack Kelly wielded over his middle daughter. Indeed Grace was to spend her life looking for her father's approval and that's from a man for whom approval was as scarce a commodity as sunshine to Scotland. Friends thought she had married Rainier in order to please him. "Frankly, my fear was she was going to get involved with this stranger just to get her father's approval," said one friend on hearing of her engagement.

The sad fact is that while Grace may have thought marrying Rainier would impress her father, this could not have been further from the truth. He was not a royalist and found his daughter's engagement to a prince bemusing at best. No bower and scraper was he: when they first met, Jack Kelly was told to address the prince as "Your Majesty" or "Your Highness." Instead he settled on the radically more informal: "Rainier." Then later, when informed of the palace protocol of allowing the prince to sit first at dinners, Jack would always pull up a pew before his princely host. You get the picture: where Grace sought reverence and respect for her prince, she got just the opposite.

Yet nothing could dampen the extravagant love she had for her father. When he became very ill with stomach pains in April 1960, she rushed to his bedside and was badly affected by his death from stomach cancer, weeks later. But despite Jack Kelly's coldness, his obvious preference for Peggy, Lizanne, and brother Kell, Grace remained devoted to him. Her following words from 1972 go some way toward an explanation: "My father was a man with tremendous personality; he had a magnetism that drew people to him. He was definitely the real focal point of our family." It was this charisma that bonded Grace to her father, that she inherited from him, but sadly he did not recognize it in his second and most successful offspring.

PAPA DON'T PREACH

If you are not the apple of your father's eye, remember, to half-borrow the title of a bestselling novel, apples are not the only fruit, so seek your counsel and inner strength elsewhere. And if Papa *does* preach, you can always do what Grace did: smile sweetly, bid him a "thank you, Daddy," and get your own way in the end, anyway.

---

*D*o also bear in mind that while we're all for you modeling yourself on Grace, you should pay heed to the times when she was wrong-footed. Like, for instance, when she allowed Jack Kelly's playing favorites with Peggy to upset her, or when she sought the approval and support she did not get from her father in the arms of older, married men. But there are some positives we can take from her relationship with Jack Kelly too, because it could be argued her unrequited paternal love was the driving force behind the blonde ambition that saw her become one of Hollywood's best-loved actresses. Of course we're not suggesting you go all out to fight with your own dear dad but if there's someone you're all out to impress, no harm in re-channeling that otherwise destructive energy and using it to fulfill a blonde, brunette, or redhead ambition of your own!

MOMMIE DEAREST

Much has been made of the effect on Grace's outlook, and even the life decisions she made, because of her relationship with her father. In fact she was, as sister Lizanne describes it in one TV interview, a "mommy's baby." Sickly, introverted Grace was often to be found tugging at Margaret's apron strings while the rest of the Kelly clan cavorted in the great outdoors, cartwheeling and roly-polying their way through childhood.

But that didn't mean that Margaret gave Grace an easy ride, particularly when it came to men. Through all her early courtships, from Don Richardson to Gene Lyons through to Oleg Cassini, "Ma Kelly" had made her feelings on the matter of her daughter's choice of man more than plain. "Mrs. Kelly had a firm jaw and a cold look," writes Oleg Cassini in his autobiography, going on to describe his attempts to warm up that coolness with his extravagant wit and charm. It didn't work. Perhaps it's hardly surprising, given her own children found her austere and strict, with Kell, mindful of her German roots, dubbing her "The Prussian General." In later life, she and Grace were close, though. Despite Margaret's misgivings over her daughter's marriage to the prince, by the mid-seventies Grace had managed the unthinkable: she had brought her mother around, impressing her with the way she had adapted to life in the palace, her child rearing, and her charity work. At last a fairy-tale ending for one relationship for our Grace.

How to Have a Good Mother-Daughter Relationship

Mothers and mothers-in-law certainly come in for a lot of stick. The butt of many jokes, they're also to blame for just about *everything* according to psychoanalysis (thanks, Herr Freud), and in recent parlance to say "your mother" is the biggest insult you can throw at anybody. Yet this is the most special of relationships; your mother knows you from womb to her tomb, and knows you like no other. Then there's the rub—perhaps sometimes "mother knows best" smarts: after all, we were "Mommy's babies" at her side for many years and then we want to cut those apron strings, while at the same time she's holding onto them madly as if they were the very umbilical cord that once joined us.

---

*W*e won't pretend to have a clue just how to conduct the perfect mother-daughter relationship (and for you men reading this, the mother-son one), but taking our cue from Grace's experience, we can say this: if both sides could just lighten up a little, dark clouds of trouble may just shift, and who knows, maybe your mother might eventually bring a little sunshine into your life?

MAMMA MIA! MOTHERS IN THE MOVIES

While fathers seldom feature in her filmography, it's striking that mothers play a key role in three of Grace's best-loved movies. Perhaps this omission is due to the fact that her male co-stars were already old enough to be her father. Grace's mother was played twice by the brilliant character actress Jessie Royce Landis, who dazzles with perfect comic timing in both *To Catch a Thief* and *The Swan*. Margalo Gillmore excels as the mother of wild child Tracy Lord in *High Society*. Still pondering that difficult mother-daughter relationship? Let's see what more we can learn about matters maternal, as we once again dip our toes into the three aforementioned films.

To Catch a Thief

The mother-daughter relationship presented in To Catch a Thief is almost the antithesis of Grace's own relationship with Ma Kelly, with the mother figure Jessie Stevens (Royce Landis) matchmaking her daughter Frances into the arms of a very bad boy indeed, in the guise of Cary Grant's ex-cat burglar, John Robie. (Imagine Margaret Kelly doing *that*!) But Ma Stevens and Ma Kelly do share a tendency to show their daughters up: "Sorry I ever sent her to finishing school—I think they finished her there" is just one line in which Royce Landis teases her daughter in front of Robie. But, unlike Ma Kelly, Ma Stevens has a playful, adventurous side, too. When her jewels go missing, she helps Frances prove that former cat burglar John Robie has not stolen them. And yes, imagine Ma Kelly doing *that*, too!

SO, WHAT CAN YOU LEARN FROM THIS MOTHER-DAUGHTER RELATIONSHIP?

Don't let Mommie Dearest drag you down if she teases you in front of a best beloved. She may just have your best interests at heart, or simply be trying to bring you out of your shell. And don't forget Grace's mother in this movie is up for an adventure, both in traveling to the Riviera with her daughter and in helping to catch the real thief. To translate this into real life, if your relationship with your own mom needs a bit of light relief, why not have your own girls' adventure or take a holiday together? I hear a little principality on the Riviera is beautiful this time of year.

The Swan

Here is an example of the pushy parent, the meddling mother, and the social climber all rolled into one: Jessie Royce Landis brilliantly reprises her role as Grace's mother as Princess Beatrix, whose days as a princess are numbered unless her daughter Alexandra marries "Europe's most eligible bachelor" Prince Albert (where have you heard that one before?) so that Beatrix can regain the throne "stolen" from her Royal European House by Napoleon. What follows is some royal matchmaking and a plot by Princess Beatrix to make Albert jealous and get him to propose, as well as a crude bit of motherly blackmail. "You have my blood in your veins, and you can't have that for nothing!" she tells Alexandra, when asking her to perform a cruel trick on the man she really loves.

SO, WHAT CAN YOU LEARN FROM THIS MOTHER-DAUGHTER RELATIONSHIP?

"Mother knows best," Princess Beatrix tells Alexandra and do you know what? Sometimes she's right. It can be galling at times, but do try and learn from the benefit of her experience. Sure, by the end of this movie Alexandra has put duty and her mother's wishes above her own happiness and we're not suggesting you take things that far, but that doesn't mean you shouldn't listen to Mother—sometimes she knows exactly what's right for you.

High Society

Margalo Gillmore plays Mrs. Seth Lord and Grace's mother in Grace's last film, the screwball musical *High Society*. It's another instance of where the parents are on the wrong side of their children, this time with Grace's character Tracy agreeing that reporters from *Spy* magazine should attend her wedding as a smokescreen for the scandal that her parents have separated. Even in the midst of her four-man muddle Tracy listens to Mother . . . but will she go for Mother's choice of man?

SO, WHAT CAN YOU LEARN FROM THIS MOTHER-DAUGHTER RELATIONSHIP?

Sometimes you've got to give Mom a break and put her best interests before yours. In so doing Tracy Lord eventually gets herself out of her love quadrangle and in the process learns much about herself. We can't help wondering if, during the filming of this movie, Grace was preoccupied with this very question, hoping her own mother would learn to approve of the fiancé to whom she would soon be wed once filming wrapped.

BRINGING UP BABIES

There's no doubting a woman with the resolve and spirit of Grace would not have agreed to a fertility test before her wedding, if baby making (in the biological sense), booties, and bonnets had not been at the very forefront of her mind. We know that when Lizanne, her younger sister, gave birth, Grace had exclaimed: "Oh, Lizanne, I want a baby!" Believe it or not, at the tender age of twenty-six, before Grace met Rainier she may have been troubled by that most dated of female dilemmas: being "left on the shelf." "For a while I was the only unmarried woman I could think of," said Grace when her career was at its peak. She was *only* twenty-six! Of course it's now unthinkable that a woman in her twenties would feel pressured to settle down, but let's remind ourselves that during the baby boom years the propaganda to conform to the stereotype of the nuclear family was immense and Grace, surrounded as she was by the world of advertising and Hollywood (both of which endorsed this stereotype), could not help but be influenced by it.

Besides, this is Grace Patricia Kelly we're talking about, a woman who liked a challenge: she'd "done" modeling, she'd "done" acting, she'd "done" movie stardom, so when the pitter-patter of tiny feet sounded with the birth of Princess Caroline in 1957 and a new challenge arose, she threw herself into the task with gusto. Prince Albert was born a year later, and Stephanie, after years when Grace suffered the heartache of a number of miscarriages, in 1965.

Whenever Grace was interviewed in later years, she was at pains to point out her principal role in Monaco was as a wife and mother. What's more, they were the roles she relished. We think it's safe to say that such enthusiasm was not Grace kowtowing to the Monaco publicity machine, but her heartfelt sentiment that family came first. Just to see the images of Grace (for instance, by her favored photographer, Howell Conant) or to hear her talking about her children in TV interviews is to know for sure that she loved motherhood. And who can blame her? All those years battling with her own family in Philadelphia, searching for Mr. Right, and enduring that troubled marriage meant nothing when here were three little people (in infancy and childhood at least!) who loved Grace unconditionally right back. In 1966, Grace told Barbara Walters: "I've had happy moments in my life, but I don't think happiness—being happy—is a perpetual state that anyone can be in; life isn't that way. But I have a certain peace of mind, yes. My children give me a great deal of happiness."

Sure, there were difficulties along the way, particularly during her daughters' teenage years. But from their cradles to her grave, Grace was a doting, attentive, and affectionate mother and Rainier, while a less-than-perfect husband, matched her in his parenting skills and style. Want to know more about the nitty-gritty of Rainier and Grace's parenting technique? Well, what are you waiting for? These top parenting tips, Grimaldi-style, won't read themselves, you know.

WHAT WOULD *Grace* DO?
BABIES AND CHILDREN

DO-IT-YOURSELF PARENTING

Despite their wealth and status Rainier and Grace kept their children close instead of packing them off to boarding school like so many other wealthy parents in their circle. Rainier himself had boarded in England from a young age and his childhood had been a sad one, colored by his parents' divorce. Given this unhappy background, Grace did not have to try too hard to encourage him to be an active and attentive parent. She herself was likewise a very hands-on parent, taking her responsibilities seriously: fretting and fussing over her children, breastfeeding each of them for three months, and later, even living with Princess Caroline in Paris during the "wild child" years. She told her biographer Donald Spoto: "We just don't like the idea of turning the children over to nannies and minders. We like to help them ourselves." In short, she did what many working mothers do: her best, but all the while fearing she was doing the opposite.

FOLLOWING IN GRACE'S FOOTSTEPS: No matter what your station in life, no matter what your schedule, make time for your kids. Read them a bedtime story (*Alice in Wonderland* was one of Grace's favorites, which she read to all three children, both in French and English, and using her superb acting skills); help them with their homework (as Grace did every afternoon); and spend time with them at the pool (OK, we don't all have our *own*, but the local pools are just as good!). Grace loathed the press attention that beset her kids and so she was delighted when Rainier found them an escape hatch: a farmhouse called Roc Angel, where the family could hide away from palace protocol and paparazzi, to be truly themselves. It's a great idea for all stressed-out parents! Sure, you may not be able to afford your own pied-à-terre in the city or country retreat, but if you've a yen to match Grace's hands-on parenting style, you can always take a bus ride into town or the country to escape the daily grind and give your kids what they want from you most: your time.

DISCIPLINE: HOW NOT TO RAISE A SPOILED BRAT

Grace believed herself to be a disciplinarian, but sadly there is much evidence that despite her best intentions, the contrary was true. She had the right idea, for certain, telling *Vogue* in 1972: "Children need discipline. They want it really. It has nothing to do with love." But other sources tell us that Grace raised a brood of spoiled children, with Stephanie in particular a royal handful, given inches and taking miles, and even being allowed to spit at visitors according to biographer Wendy Leigh! That said, Grace *did* discipline her kids. In her 1985 interview with Barbara Walters, Princess Caroline recalled that while Grace never spanked Albert, she did spank Caroline, and one time when Caroline bit Albert, Grace bit her right back!

FOLLOWING IN GRACE'S FOOTSTEPS: Is there such a thing as *too much* love for your children? Grace's lifelong friend and bridesmaid Rita Gam would say yes: "Grace almost over-adored her children." Of course, with a disinterested husband and having given up her career, it's not hard to see why she made her children the focal point of her life. Here's another example of where we can learn from one of Grace's less sure-footed moves: love your children, but don't spoil them; make sure you keep up other interests and don't become too child-centric. OK, we're not all raising little princes and princesses, but we don't want them to act like it either!

HAND-ME-DOWN PARENTING

Grace tried her hardest to be a good mother, but by bringing up her kids "in the American way," which she describes as being a little more laissez-faire than the European style, combined with her children's royal status, made for a heady (and tantrum-like) combination. Talking about her children in her 1982 interview with ABC's Pierre Salinger, Grace said: "I've tried to instill a lot of my own upbringing into their lives." Strange, wouldn't you say? Despite the tug-of-war relationship with her father, despite the Kelly parents' vetting of her partners, despite the austere, almost loveless relationship, Grace wanted to take something of that discipline, of the Kelly family's traditional household roles, and impart that to her own kids. As she related to *Vogue* in 1972: "The father should be the leader of the family. He's physically stronger—and for a reason. It's nature's way of showing who should be leader. The woman is the homemaker. It's up to her to create the cadre, the framework of family life."

FOLLOWING IN GRACE'S FOOTSTEPS: Think back to your own childhood and even if this was not the happiest of times, try and conjure up an image of what your parents did well so that you can replicate this with your own kids. Of course, you may do so simply by osmosis and that's all good. Equally, even if you make a conscious effort not to do so, you may replicate the mistakes of your parents' past. It's only natural to find yourself turning into your mother or father. Grace did, and we're afraid such is life! As for the traditional roles espoused by Grace . . . well, we're talking about a woman born in 1929, and nearly 100 years later we're not entirely in agreement about Dad being the leader of the family pack. You may have your own views on that, though.

TEENAGE TORPOR

The teenage years were not easy ones for Caroline and Stephanie, whose "wild child" status was magnified for the whole world to see in the pages of glossy magazines throughout the 1970s. Rainier would later say that his two girls "have a great mind of their own—they're very stubborn." Who'd have thought it? Willful, stubborn, headstrong Grace raising two similarly willful, stubborn, headstrong girls? And here's where Grace's past came back to haunt her, not least when it came to *affaires de coeur*. "How can I bring up my daughters not to have an affair with a married man when I was having affairs with married men all the time?" she would tell a friend in the 1970s. So what did Grace do here? Did she lay down the law, swapping those white gloves for an iron fist? No way! She was sensible, proffered advice when requested, kept her children close, and—persuaded by her husband—did not stand in the way when Caroline wished to marry playboy Phillipe Junot in 1978 (and she was also at her side when the pair divorced in 1980, with no boasts of "Told you so!").

FOLLOWING IN GRACE'S FOOTSTEPS: Teenagers . . . who'd have them? Well, sure as night follows day, your once bouncing, bonny, ever-loving cherubs will soon turn into hormonally challenged, independence-bound, sexually curious teenagers. We hope when our own children reach those difficult years we'll be equal to Grace and Rainier's parenting technique, sticking as they did to Caroline, Stephanie, and Albert through thick and thin. And, as advice for all those rearing teenagers, we feel that we can't do better than that.

chapter nine

Friends for Life

"Grace is just herself, and anyone who meets her falls in love with her."
WALLY WESTMORE, MAKEUP ARTIST AND GRACE'S FRIEND

L UCKY FOR GRACE, AS the saying goes, you don't choose your family but you do choose your friends, and choose them she did: wisely, with great instinct, and in abundance. Indeed she counted a constellation of Hollywood stars among her best friends, and even though she could not, because of her status, become true friends with anyone from the Monégasque community, later in life she continued to bedazzle all those she met—whether on an airplane, in the palace, or at a charity event, Grace's innate wit and warmth seemed to attract friendship like a moth to a flame.

In this chapter on her nearest and dearest we'll provide a few hints and tips on how you can match Grace's own friendship style, what to do when the boundary between friends and lovers becomes blurred, and how, like Grace, you can cheer family and friends by hosting the most swellegant, elegant parties imaginable.

MAKE FRIENDS, NEVER BREAK FRIENDS

In the grand circles in which Grace Kelly moved, one might have believed that true friendships would be unthinkable, as those Hollywood shark-types waded around one another in the shallow depths of competitiveness, their friendships fueled by rivalry, gossip, and one-upmanship. Not so. Grace made firm friends with many of her co-stars throughout her career, although her closest friends were those she made in New York and her years before Hollywood.

Possibly her best female friend from the Hollywood years was Ava Gardner. The pair had bonded on the set of *Mogambo* (1953), as Grace counseled Ava through filming while she and then husband Frank Sinatra fought like (big) cat and dog in the jungle. The two women were chalk and cheese: Gardner overtly sexual, a drinker, and from a difficult background whereas Kelly was the ice queen, the bad drinker (in the 1950s, at least), and the Philadelphia socialite. Opposites attract, so they say, and the pair became lifelong friends after their African adventure: "She was a great lady," Gardner would say, "and also great fun."

There's that word "fun" again. How different from the pristine and prissy, white-gloved image that the media presented of Grace in the mid-fifties. And yet when those closest to her recall her character, that word "fun" is repeated time and again. "I don't know how such a fun-loving girl stays married to that fuddy-duddy," Cary Grant once said. Of her co-stars, Kelly's friendship with Grant was one of the most enduring. He and his wife, Betsy, gifted Grace her beloved pet poodle, Oliver, shortly before she set sail for her wedding. They were there for key moments in Grace's life: her wedding, the ball held for Princess Caroline's wedding in 1978, Grace and Rainier's twenty-fifth wedding anniversary, and Grace's funeral.

One of Grace's most extraordinary friendships was with the singer Josephine Baker. In the early 1950s when racial tensions were still high in the United States and the civil rights movement was in its infancy, Baker had been denied entrance to the famous Stork Club, where Kelly was dining with friends. Scandalized, Grace stormed out of the venue with her fellow diners and never ate there again. She and Baker were friends thereafter, and when Grace learned of Josephine's bankruptcy in Paris in the early 1970s, together with Jackie Onassis she helped finance her comeback, as well as providing a roof for her and Baker's twelve adopted children.

Besides her close girlfriends, the Hollywood A-list, and other showbiz pals, Grace Kelly made friends with people the world over: on her travels, through her work, and simply in her daily life. She befriended those from nobility and high-ranking politicians (Winston Churchill was fond of her), as well as everyday folk. Despite her best efforts, she did not make friends with any of her subjects, though. "The princess's idea of inviting local people to dinner parties was not a success," observed Rainier. Small wonder she remained steadfast and true to her old friends, keeping in regular contact with Rita Gam, Judith Quine, and Charlotte Winston, among others, even when living the high life in Monte Carlo.

LESSONS FROM LA GRACE IN MAKING TRUE AND LASTING FRIENDSHIPS

LESSON ONE: MAKE FRIENDS FROM ALL WALKS OF LIFE

As we've seen, it was not for want of trying that Grace did not make new friends in Monaco, but elsewhere she attracted friends as easily as bees make honey. For instance, she met restaurateur Jim McMullen on a transatlantic flight and became fast friends with the writer Gwen Robyns at the Palace of Monaco while persuading her not to write a planned biography of her life. (Robyns never did, and the pair remained true friends from then on.) The message is clear: look beyond your circle—heck, you may even want to buddy up with a few squares! Friends come in all shapes and sizes, and you never know what new friendships you may strike up unless you get chatting.

LESSON TWO: REMEMBER BIRTHDAYS

As a proud Scorpio, who was also interested in astrology (see also page 206), birthdays were important to Grace. While shooting *Mogambo* in the African jungle, the entire cast and crew toasted both of the female leads' birthdays: Grace's on November 12 and Ava's on Christmas Eve. After that, according to Gardner: "No matter where I was in the world, every year a birthday present arrived from Grace. She never forgot. . . ." If you find it hard to keep up with birthdays, why not buy a calendar especially as a reminder?

Purchase greeting cards and stamps in advance; then all you have to do is pop on a stamp and post the card closer to the time. Friends will love and remember you for this kind action, and who knows, maybe next year your own doormat will be swamped with cards in return.

LESSON THREE: KEEP IN TOUCH

Grace was a prolific letter writer. Indeed, her warm words to family and friends have given her biographers an insight to her thoughts and feelings throughout her life, but they also reveal that her loved ones were often in her thoughts. Now in this age of instant communication there's really no excuse not to stay in touch with friends by e-mail, face-to-face using Skype, or by telephone. But to be a friend with true Grace, why not pen a letter to show you really care? To finish this section (and in case letter writing makes you think of the classroom), here are a few notes on how to pen or type that perfect missive:

○ Think of the last time you met your pal and include a fond memory of that occasion. Ask questions and provide food for thought so that you gain a response.

○ Take a tip from *Debrett's*, the kings and queens of etiquette: "Writing by hand focuses the mind. There is no delete button, no backspace, so words must be considered and chosen carefully before being committed to paper, making their meaning all the more succinct."

○ Don't be shy about sharing big secrets by letter or sending important news—they become all the more exciting when dropped through the letterbox instead of dashed off by e-mail.

○ Love letters might seem *so* last century but a billet-doux is, in fact, so intimate, so personal, so, well, *racy*! Let's not forget that Rainier and Grace's entire courtship was played out in epistolary form. Oh, to be the ink on one of *those* letters and privy to the buildup of their big romance! The trick here is to pen your letter, hand-on-heart—figuratively speaking, of course. During her courtship with Oleg Cassini, Grace's message to him was simple: "I want to be your wife."

○ Sign off with a warm greeting. Grace liked to use "with deepest affection" or "much love."

○ One final note: don't write to receive! Judith Quine would say of Grace: "No admonitions for not writing, though letters from her pals were very important to her."

WHEN GRACE MET DAVID . . .
AND GRAHAM . . . AND ROBERT . . .

Though most of Grace's friendships were with women, she also enjoyed a number of longstanding friendships with the male variety of the species, including the actor David Niven. But was she "just good friends" with Niven, or indeed the sprinkling of younger men she met in middle age? Well, here's another area of Grace's life that her biographers put under the microscope and make a mountain out of an amoeba.

There's no question that Grace and David Niven had an affair in the mid-1950s: they'd met on the MGM lot and were immediately attracted to the other's sparkling wit and good humor. Then, later, when Niven bought a house across the bay from Monaco in Cap Ferrat in the early 1960s, much time was spent together in the company of other Hollywood stars. "The actor David Niven shared her love of banter. There were gales of laughter every time he visited the palace," her former PA Louisette Levy-Soussan Azzoaglio recalled in a 2010 interview. Meanwhile, Niven's own son Jamie has often confirmed that the pair enjoyed a close and lasting friendship. Certain Hollywood insiders would claim that relationship went further: "It was a last hurrah for both of them," one recounts. "It wasn't just a fling. It went on for many years, until her death."

So, were Grace and David simply good friends? Both are no longer with us to reveal the truth (and it's not our place to say), but it would seem extraordinary, given the rumors of other affairs Grace was meant to be having around the same time. For, in middle age, she had befriended a sprinkling of younger men who she, with her usual wit, referred to as her "toy boys." There was Robert Dornhelm, director of *The Children of Theatre Street* (for which Grace provided the narration); then there was academic and playboy Graham Binns, with whom Grace danced the night away (and some would say more) at a party hosted by Elizabeth and Richard Burton in 1972; also restaurateur Jim McMullen, whom she met on a transatlantic flight. Platonic or not, Grace got a kick out of these relationships. "What she wanted was glamour, and those young men supplied it," her friend Gwen Robyns would later say. And with Rainier off gallivanting with the young and beautiful, who can blame her? Sometimes, just sometimes, needs must be met.

186 · What Would Grace Do?

JUST GOOD FRIENDS

So, can men and women be "just good friends," or if we are to mirror Grace should there always be an extra frisson of je ne sais quoi in our friendships with the opposite sex? The simple answer is, it's entirely up to you! Nevertheless, it doesn't hurt to lay down a few ground rules for male/female friendships, minefields though these may be:

RULE ONE: When your male friend is attached, don't proffer him relationship advice or have a bad word to say about his dear lady friend/wife. If you want to stay good friends, treat her as an extension of him.

RULE TWO: If you secretly have feelings for the friend in question, bear in mind these wise words from Harry (Billy Crystal) of *When Harry Met Sally* (1989) fame: "Men and women can't be friends because the sex part always gets in the way." But this is only true if you harbor lustful feelings for him. Speaking of harbors, if those lustful feelings *do* exist and you are already in an intimate relationship, jump ship from the friendship before it's too late!

RULE THREE: Discretion is the better part of valor. In other words, don't share intimate secrets about your lover/relationship with your male pals (particularly those of the sexual variety, or any you wouldn't share with a girlfriend).

RULE FOUR: Alcohol is your own worst enemy if there's a certain spark between you. Loose lips sink ships, and alcohol makes lips even looser. If you want to hang out with a gorgeous male pal, why not choose a more refined outing such as a visit to a museum or a daytime stroll?

RULE FIVE: If you want to be friends with your ex, there is one simple rule: don't, just *don't*! Though Grace kept in touch with Don Richardson by letter, her most high-profile exes, including Oleg Cassini and Jean-Pierre Aumont, were certainly not on the Palace of Monaco's Christmas card list. It's a Grace Kelly precedent that you would be well advised to follow.

A VERY SPECIAL RELATIONSHIP

"Mr. Hitchcock taught me everything about cinema."

GRACE KELLY

"There's no one else like her in Hollywood."

ALFRED HITCHCOCK

She was the high society beauty brought up on Philadelphia's affluent Main Line, while he was the son of a blue collar, humble East End poultry dealer. A love of moving pictures and relentless talent, but more superficially a stunning head of blonde hair, brought them together. Over an intense two-year period, the pair made three pictures together, establishing a lifelong May-to-December friendship.

Speaking of months, Grace was definitely the flavor of Hitch's, with this also being a relationship of unrequited infatuation. Notoriously prone to falling for his leading ladies (Ingrid Bergman and Madeleine Carroll before Grace), Hitchcock was also fascinated by the filmic opportunities offered by blondes, of whom he said: "Blondes make the best victims. They're like virgin snow that shows up the bloody footprints." In Grace, he had found his ultimate blonde and his ultimate leading lady, responding to the simmering sexuality beneath her ice maiden exterior as eagerly as a teenage boy might to a more overt display of eroticism. In fact, fulsome as this may sound, Hitchcock would have loved to have cast Grace in each one of his movies requiring a leading lady after *Dial M for Murder*.

It's a rare skill to spot talent from one movie test alone, but Hitchcock did just that with Grace. On seeing her test for the movie *Taxi*, he fell hook, line, and sinker for her cool exterior blended with that inner passion, immediately engaging her for *Dial M for Murder* without having seen any of her previous movies. "From the *Taxi* test you could see Grace's potential for restraint," he later said. "I always tell actors don't use the face for nothing. Grace has this control. It's a rare thing for a girl at such an age." It was the start of a very special relationship and the director's high expectations of Grace were proved right when she displayed her sharp intelligence and instincts in all three of the movies on which they worked. In a later interview Hitchcock revealed to François Truffaut that he so trusted and admired talented Grace that he had given her more to do in each of the movies made with him. "To build up Grace Kelly," he said, "in each picture between *Dial M for Murder* and *To Catch a Thief*, we made her role a more interesting one."

Hardworking and eager to improve her craft, Grace found that being Hitchcock's protégée proved immeasurably helpful. "It was thanks to him that I understood that murder scenes should be shot like love scenes and love scenes like murder scenes," she said. The special relationship was a two-way street.

A friendship flourished off set, too. Hitchcock taught Grace how to use a Super 8 camera, which she used to make home movies of her family and friends. They also shared a sense of humor: when the director taunted Grace with innuendo and raunch, she gave as good as she got, saying she'd heard worse at her convent school. But a more potent emotion also blossomed from the flower of their friendship: in Grace, Hitchcock found a girl he adored and he thought he could shape into his ultimate blonde fantasy woman. Quite simply, he was in love. Even if his feelings were akin to "a schoolboy crush" and he knew his lust would not go anywhere, this only made Grace's remoteness all the more alluring.

---

*W*hat about you? Is there a special relationship in your life that brings out the best in you, or has the potential to? Are you someone's muse, providing the backbone to their creativity, or perhaps you're the creative one and need to seek out a muse of your own? Careful, though: there's a fine line, as the partnership between Hitchcock and Grace showed, between inspiration and adoration, so don't allow the waters to become muddied if you happen to be already attached.

THE MARNIE STORY

The mutual appreciation society was genuine and heartfelt, hence Hitchcock's heartbreak when Grace left for Monaco and his attempts to lure her back to Hollywood at the earliest opportunity. In 1962, he invited Grace to play the part of the eponymous Marnie and she leapt at the chance. With his triumphant political machinations that same year, even Rainier was in a jubilant mood and gave his blessing to his wife taking up the part. But there was one more character in this story about the casting of *Marnie* (the villain of the piece, if you will) and this collective character was the people of Monaco: they responded with complete shock to the idea of their princess playing a kleptomaniac, and one with a very shady past indeed. So, that was that: Grace's chance of returning to Hollywood was kiboshed.

But there were no hard feelings: Grace and Hitchcock's friendship continued apace. Indeed their correspondence, some of which has gone on display at various exhibitions, shows them to have had a brilliant rapport. Whenever she could, Grace was there to support Hitchcock's career when it was celebrated. For instance, at a black-tie gala to celebrate his oeuvre in April 1974, she was one of the actresses who introduced his work with a short speech. Hitchcock died of renal failure at his Bel Air home in 1980, two years before his ultimate blonde became a victim—not in the snow, but on the very hilltops where he'd captured her rare cinematic qualities in *To Catch a Thief*, almost twenty-five years previously.

HITCHCOCK BLONDES

After Grace, a number of elegant derrières perched on Hitchcock's casting couch in the hope of becoming his new leading lady, but Grace's "rejection" deeply upset him, and from that point on, his blondes would come in for some harsh treatment. Variously pecked by birds, stabbed in showers, and thrown from church steeples, they could only hope for the relatively less gruesome state of being just "victims in the snow." But who were they? Can you match the Hitchcock Blondes on the following page to the movies in which they starred?

North by Northwest	Kim Novak
Vertigo	Tippi Hedren
Marnie	Eva Marie Saint

Answers:

Marnie (1964)—Tippi Hedren
This particular movie was not a hit with cinemagoers. Film critic François Truffaut has even suggested that it was a turning point for the worse in the Master of Suspense's career. Hitchcock had put Tippi Hedren under an exclusive contract to work with him alone—quite an exceptional state of affairs, even for the 1950s. But after her ill treatment by him during the filming of Marnie, and before it on the set of The Birds, she refused ever to work with him again. Simply put, she was weirded out by his attempts to fashion her as the new Grace Kelly and would later claim that he had ruined her career.

Vertigo (1958)—Kim Novak
Before Tippi Hedren, Hitchcock tried out another actress as his Kelly doppelgänger: Kim Novak. And it's perhaps Novak in Vertigo who most spookily resembles Grace. This was an unsettling movie, described by Hitchcock as "the hero's attempts to re-create the image of a dead woman through another who's alive," and produces all sorts of uncomfortable parallels between Hitchcock's blonde fetish and his Dr. Frankenstein–like attempts to create a new Grace Kelly.

North by Northwest (1959)—Eva Marie Saint
A star in her own right, she was best known for her 1954 debut in On the Waterfront (for which she won an Academy Award for Best Supporting Actress) when Hitchcock cast her to star as Eve Kendall alongside Cary Grant (Roger Thornhill) in North by Northwest. The suspense thriller proved a great vehicle for her sophisticated, ice-cool good looks. Now, why do those words ring bells? But Saint is no second-rate Grace Kelly: as a double agent and femme fatale to Cary Grant's "everyman," she's second to none, we believe. Fortunately, critics at the time agreed and her performance was lauded in Hollywood and beyond.

THE HOSTESS WITH THE MOSTESS

Though Grace was at times somewhat shy and introverted, she adored having family and friends to stay at the Palace of Monaco. During their visits, she loved to smuggle a little taste of back home into Monte Carlo, hosting old-fashioned American barbecues around the pool that she had installed at the palace and at the same time blowing out the cobwebs of some rather stuffy traditions. Grace's hospitality was renowned and any friend or family member had an open invitation to stay chez Grimaldi.

Not all of her hospitality had such an apple pie homeliness to it, though. Her position as Grace, Princess of Monaco, and as a charity organizer meant she also threw some lavish dinners and balls. And of course where would a Hollywood goddess be, if not clinking glasses and surrounded by merriment at a classic 1950s cocktail party?

Now we'll take a quick peek at all the ingredients you need to host two of these events, without so much as breaking into a very un-Grace-like sweat.

HOW TO THROW A SWELL PARTY I: THE 1950s COCKTAIL PARTY

What frills, what frocks!
What furs, what rocks!
What gaiety!

COLE PORTER, AS SUNG BY FRANK SINATRA IN *HIGH SOCIETY*

The 1950s—a time when men could hold their liquor and even if they didn't, they drank in abundance; when ladies were just that, and hats and gloves at a cocktail party were de rigueur. In those days the cocktail hour started at 5 p.m. and ended with the last man or woman standing. This was a time when half measures didn't really exist and it's in this spirit that we invite you to host a Grace Kelly–esque cocktail party. So much the better if you happen to be clutching an Oscar, or other hard-won award!

THE DRINKS

French champagne is a must if you wish to hold a swellegant, elegant affair à la *High Society*; cocktails even more so. Vodka Martinis, Whiskey Sours, and Tom Collins are all classic 1950s drinks to serve, or why not try something a little more special? To mark the occasion of the 2010

A "High Society"

3 Tbsp. gin
1½ Tbsp. lemon juice
1 Tbsp. homemade raspberry
    syrup
2 tsp. pasteurized egg white

Put all the ingredients in a shaker filled with ice cubes. Shake, shake, shake, and strain into a chilled martini glass.

Grace Kelly: Style Icon exhibition at London's Victoria and Albert Museum, award-winning mixologist Agostino Perrone devised three unique Grace Kelly cocktails to be served in the Connaught Bar. We smack our lips at the sound of the "High Society." If you do decide to go down this swanky avenue, have someone attend the bar who knows one end of a Caipirinha from another, and make sure it's well stocked to avert a drinks disaster.

"My nerves could use a drink."

FRANCES "FRANCIE" STEVENS IN *TO CATCH A THIEF*

THE FOOD

At this kind of party, food plays a supporting role to your superstar guest: the cocktails. But serve a little nourishment you must to line the stomachs of your guests, and canapés and little bite-sized treats are the only thing that will make the grade. Smoked salmon blinis are very easy to whip up; good Serrano or Parma ham is even easier. The tapas options from Spanish and Middle Eastern cuisine are not only beautiful but great for vegetarian guests. A cake is a nice idea for a Ta-Da! moment later on in the evening, if it's a special occasion. When the Kellys threw a party for Grace and Rainier's engagement, a lavish cake took center stage, and what about the elaborate Scorpio cake for Grace's fortieth? Think big, think theme, and think cake!

THE DRESS CODE

More is *more*. Shimmering cocktail gowns, prom dresses that tease and float, and evening gowns that scream "Grace Kelly" are all permitted. If you can go vintage, please do so, but bear in mind our hints and tips in chapter four (see pages 79–100). Then all you need to do is sweep your hair up into a chignon, add a fascinator or a hat, and practice standing up straight in your heels, particularly if you plan to imbibe several Tom Collins.

HOW TO HAVE A SWELL PARTY II: THE BACKYARD BARBECUE

If cocktail parties aren't your bag, or you wish to hold a more low-key family affair, try a backyard barbecue. Most supermarkets now sell little disposable ones if you don't own a barbecue, so there's really no excuse.

THE DRINKS

Pitchers of beer, bowls of punch, and bottles of rosé will keep the big kids happy; Coca-Cola from the classic glass bottles for the little ones (just remember the straws). Heck, hand them out to the adults, too—nothing like drinking Coke from a bottle to take you back to your own childhood or to conjure up a redolent image of a 1950s happy family.

THE FOOD

Hey, it's a barbecue so get those charcoals burning and grill a whole heap of burgers, hot dogs, and steaks! For an authentic American backyard barbecue taste, serve a baked bean casserole and one gelatin mold salad. If you're not quite ready for the full vintage food revival, homemade coleslaw is a nice touch and so much tastier than store-bought. And don't forget the condiments!

THE DRESS CODE

Even when residing in Monaco, Grace took great pride in being an American and in 1966, she held an "American Week" in Monte Carlo. There was even a barbecue party at the Mont Agel Golf Course, where Grace was seen sporting shorts and a baseball cap. Yes, *really*! So different to her usual style, but sometimes we all have to kick back and relax with family and friends, and Grace was no different.

---

*T*he message is clear: if you want to be on the same page as Grace in the hospitality department, invite all your friends with open arms. But remember the old proverb: after three days, fish and guests begin to smell. And if you're not one to go to the bother of planning a big shindig, you'd do well to remember the words of one Mrs. Dorothy L. Parker: "If you wear a short enough skirt, the party will come to you!" Not that Grace would raise her hemline, you understand, but with her fondness for the bawdy, we're sure this would raise a polite titter!

Grace Kelly's

Little Black Book

SHOP

NEW YORK

Ann Taylor
645 Madison Avenue
New York, NY 10022
212-832-9114
www.anntaylor.com

Bloomingdale's
1000 Third Avenue
New York, NY 10022
212-705-2000
www.bloomingdales.com

Banana Republic Flagship Store
Rockefeller Center
626 Fifth Avenue
New York, NY 10020
212-974-2350
www.bananarepublic.com

GAP Flagship Store
1212 Sixth Avenue
New York, NY 10036
212-730-1087
www.gap.com

J.Crew
91 Fifth Avenue
New York, NY 10003
212-255-4848
www.jcrew.com

LONDON

Jo Malone
23 Brook Street
London
W1K 4HA
0870 192 5181
www.jomalone.co.uk

LONDON

Selfridges & Co.
400 Oxford Street
London
W1A 1AB
0113 369 8040
www.selfridges.com

Marks and Spencer Flagship Store
458 Oxford Street
London
W1C 1AP
020 7935 7954
www.marksandspencer.com

Lulu Guinness
23 Royal Exchange
Threadneedle Street
London
EC3V 3LR
020 7626 5391
www.luluguinness.com

Smythson
40 New Bond Street
London
W1S 2DE
020 7629 8558
www.smythson.com

PARIS

Galeries Lafayette
40 Blvd Haussmann
75009 Paris
01 42 82 34 56
www.galerieslafayette.com

Hermès
42 Avenue George V
75008 Paris
01 47 20 48 51
www.hermes.com

Chanel
42 Avenue Montaigne
75008 Paris
01 47 23 74 12
www.chanel.com

Comptoir des Cotonniers
10 Rue du Jour
75001 Paris
01 53 40 75 77
www.comptoirdescotonniers.com

SOCIAL

NEW YORK

The Cort Theatre
138 West 48th Street
New York, NY 10036
212-944-3700

Grace trod the boards here to play "the daughter" in Strindberg's *The Father* in 1949. The theater remains a Broadway theater-lover's destination.

LONDON

The Royal Opera House
Covent Garden
London
WC2E 9DD
020 7240 1200

PARIS

Théâtre des Champs-Élysées
15 Avenue Montaigne
75008 Paris
01 53 23 99 19

Princess Grace of Monaco made her first public appearance without Rainier at this grand old theater in the early 1970s.

MONTE CARLO

Théâtre Princesse Grace
12 Avenue d'Ostende
Monaco
93 25 32 27

This is the theater that Grace had restored to its former glory in 1981, and which Rainier had named after her following her death.

SOCIAL

NEW YORK

Le Veau d'Or
129 East 60th Street
New York, NY 10022
212-838-8133

Oleg Cassini relentlessly pursued
Grace after running into her here in
the early 1950s. It remains a favored
restaurant of New Yorkers due to its
timeless elegance.

"21" Club
21 West 52nd Street
New York, NY 10019
212-582-7200

Lisa Carol Fremont (Grace Kelly)
has "21" deliver dinner to a laid-up
L. B. "Jeff" Jefferies (James Stewart)
in *Rear Window*.

LONDON

Café de Paris
3-4 Coventry Street
London
W1D 6BL
020 7734 7700

This gorgeous Grade II listed
building on Piccadilly Circus was
one of Grace's favorite restaurants.
It now hosts a number of themed
evenings and is more for the
tourists.

PARIS

Maxim's de Paris
3 Rue Royale
75008 Paris
01 42 65 27 94

In the 1950s Maxim's was quite the
place to be seen with movie stars
such as Marlene Dietrich being one
of their patrons. Brigitte Bardot
even caused a scandal when she
entered the famous restaurant in
bare feet!

SLEEP

NEW YORK

Waldorf Astoria
301 Park Avenue
New York, NY 10022
212-355-3000

Here Grace and Rainier celebrated their engagement with a fabulous ball.

LONDON

The Savoy
The Strand
London
WC2R 0EU
020 7836 4343

Grace's bed for the night when she pursued Clark Gable after filming *Mogambo*.

PARIS

Hotel Raphael
17 Avenue Kléber
75116 Paris
01 53 64 32 00

Jean-Pierre Aumont and Grace stole a few nights here (in adjoining suites) during their brief courtship in the late spring of 1955.

MAJORCA, SPAIN

Playa de Formentor
Carrer de Formentor 3
07470 Pollença
Majorca, Spain
971 89 91 00

In 1956, Grace Kelly and Prince Rainier spent their honeymoon sailing, dining, and wine tasting in Majorca. This was their choice of hotel when moored.

FRENCH RIVIERA

InterContinental Carlton Cannes
58 Blvd de la Croisette
Cannes 06414
04 93 06 40 06

The central location for *To Catch a Thief*. Grace also stayed here during the Cannes film festival in 1955—when she first met Rainier.

chapter ten

Legacy

*"I'd like to be remembered as being a decent human being,
and a caring one."*

GRACE PATRICIA KELLY

T HERE IS A POLITICAL saying from the French, known as the *entente cordiale*, when two countries previously at odds gain a new
understanding of each other's position and form an allegiance. In
the early 1980s it might be said that Grace and Rainier were enjoying something of a personal *entente cordiale*, as Rainier's absorption
in finance and politics was on the wane, and he had softened his
attitude toward Grace's past and her Hollywood connections. However, it would be exaggerating to say they had achieved "True Love"
suggestive of the boat on which Grace had sailed with Bing Crosby
in *High Society*. It was more of the kind of understanding reached
by that other Crosby/Kelly pairing in *The Country Girl*: one based
on mutual respect, friendship, and bonding over a shared strength
through adversity; in Grace and Rainier's case through the political
and economic difficulties in Monaco, through the trials and tribula-
tions of bringing up children, and, buoyed by their successful

twenty-fifth wedding anniversary celebrations, through twenty-five years of a less-than-perfect marriage.

During this period, despite suffering personally from the physical woes of menopause, or the "angry jaws" as Grace termed it, she was enjoying something of a second wind in her career. She was giving poetry readings at international festivals, had been involved in a number of films (even acting in one), and continued her involvement with cultural activity and charity work in the principality and beyond. At the dawn of her fifties the mood was positive: soon the last of her children would be finishing high school, a certain freedom from old routines was on the horizon, and Grace was looking out as a sailor might, surveying a new land. Excitement, new opportunities, and adventure were all planned, and even, with Rainier's blessing, the possibility of making a movie of her own. How cruel then was the fate that saw her car crash not far from Roc Angel, the family farm, on September 13, 1982. As our story comes to an end, in this chapter we won't dwell on the details of Grace's tragic accident, no historical rubberneckers are we. Instead we'll celebrate her life and legacy, and as we tip our hats (or should that be stylish hats?), we'll consider our own legacies, too.

DESTINY'S CHILD

Throughout this book, the aim has been to give you an insight into what made Grace Kelly tick: passion in abundance, deep reserves of love for her family, friends, and lovers, conscientiousness, professionalism, perfectionism, even. But there's an aspect of her character that we've neglected to assess and before we go on to look at her legacy, it's time to redress this and look at her mystical side and her superstition.

Here's yet another contradiction surrounding our leading lady: on the one hand there was her Catholicism, on the other her love of astrology and tarot and a fondness for a tome called *The Pursuit of Destiny*. Do you regard such things as being hocus-pocus? Well, Grace didn't. In fact, such was the strength of her belief in astrology that for her fortieth birthday, she threw that elegant Scorpio-themed ball. Being a Scorpio had always been important to Grace, so throwing a ball for just Scorpios and their partners for her big birthday was a no-brainer. Elizabeth Taylor and Richard Burton were there, as was David Niven, while portraits of historical Scorpios such as Edgar Allan Poe and Marie-Antoinette hung on the ballroom walls. The pièce de résistance was a giant cake with golden Scorpio decorations. This interest in astrology was not a symptom of a midlife crisis, though: even in her twenties Grace had been a star fascinated by, well, the stars and very proud of her sign being in the sun of Scorpio.

Grace believed herself to be a typical Scorpio: highly sexed, hugely passionate, yet pragmatic, too. Scorpios are also creative types, with ardor and energy in abundance. And what about those Scorpio eyes? Grace's piercing baby-blue peepers certainly live up to the reputation of a Scorpio's eyes being their most alluring and powerful physical trait. Basically, she believed in the stars' influence on our lives and their ability to shape our personalities, and was certainly guided by her horoscope when it came to making schemes and plans.

What a contradiction in comparison to her very traditional Roman Catholic faith, of which her biographer Donald Spoto said in 2010: "Her faith was enormously important to her. It wasn't that sort of superstitious, knee-jerk, frightened, guilt-ridden kind of Irish-American Catholicism. It was very deep. It was tolerant. It was open." But it was not faith but tarot cards, astrology, and palmistry that Grace used as a tool to see her through darker days; she used all these techniques of divination to contemplate her present and to allow her future to be read. A strong believer in fate, she gave herself over to it, even when it came to choosing her marriage partner. Remember her words when asked about the sudden, mad rush toward marriage to Rainier? "It's my destiny," she said.

ORACULAR SPECTACULAR

So, what's your destiny? Have you ever had a vision that augurs what lies ahead? Do you see your future in the lap of the gods, the cards, or the stars? Or do you regard your destiny as something more within your own control, thank you very much? Whether you're a no-nonsense non-believer or devout about divination, there's something to be said for using various disciplines of fortune telling as a kind of thinking therapy. They allow time for rumination on both your character and your future, and can be a useful tool to assess where you are in life. So, you're not that well versed when it comes to the divination department? Let's take a quick look at Grace's preferred methods and you'll soon recognize your shaman from your charlatans.

Astrology

Astrologers believe that the movements and relative positions of celestial bodies can be interpreted and have an influence on human affairs and the natural world. Grace put her faith in astrology: she would always read her horoscope and had her birth chart read many times in order to find out more about what lay ahead. In her youth she was very fond of a book of astrological charts called *The Pursuit of Destiny*, which claimed to predict the future. The book's chart for

Grace revealed that her destiny would be effortless; she would rarely have to fight her way to the next stage in life and others would help her along the way. Significantly, it also stated: "Scorpio should never end up with a Gemini, the pair are not suitable for one another." Her cries of dismay when she discovered that Rainier was himself a Gemini could probably have been heard from the heavens themselves. In fact, her preference was for Leos and of course her fellow sign of Scorpio, but by the early 1980s, she had "found a way to get along with a Gemini," she told a lifelong friend.

Tarot

The tarot is a set of seventy-eight picture cards used by Romani and other mystical types for fortune telling. Grace loved to read her friends' tarot cards and was even said to be reading people's cards on the *Constitution*, the ship that took her all the way from New York to Monaco in 1956. Reading the tarot is fun and relatively simple to do, once you have learned the meanings of each of the cards. They are laid out in formation (the most common being a Celtic cross) to read a person's past, present, and future, each card having its own meaning, including the much-feared death (which doesn't mean death in the literal sense). There are an infinite number of packs to choose from, each with their own distinct illustrations. If you'd like to try them out, you could do no worse than get hold of the Hollywood tarot pack online, where a glamorous photo of Grace is used to represent the "Snow Queen," that is the Queen of Cups.

Parapsychology

Of all her superstitions, perhaps Grace's strongest one was the belief that she possessed ESP. She was once tested for this in Monaco and was shown to have some talent as a psychic. Rainier was often fond of joking that if he were ever allowed to gamble in Monaco's casinos, his wife should be at his side. Grace was said to have ESP about men in particular, with an ability to read what was on their minds. And she famously made one extraordinary prediction about her own life: that she would one day die in a car crash. This has been noted by many of her biographers, perhaps the most compelling piece of evidence contained in Wendy Leigh's biography *True Grace*, where Leigh reveals that in the mid-seventies Grace had consulted a psychic, Frank Andrews, and they had discussed her premonition that she was going to die in a car crash.

The fact that Grace, in so many ways a pragmatist, was a lover of the so-called dark arts is not so surprising when we think of other aspects of her personality: intelligent, bright, and questioning; it's no wonder she had a propensity to wonder what was around the corner. As a perfectionist, constantly trying to better herself, she used tools such as the tarot to help her look deeper into what made her the person she was. And with all those hours spent alone in the Palace of Monaco, she had time to brood over her past, present, and future. How interesting it might have been to be a fly on the wall as she studied her palm or her birth chart, and to know exactly what she was searching for. Just what was it that Grace wanted the answers to?

GRACE, HOPES, AND CHARITY

As we've discussed throughout this book, Grace worked hard for Monaco and its people, also for charities throughout the world even when her children were small. In 1958, soon after the birth of Prince Albert, she became chairman of Monaco's Red Cross and would hold an annual ball to raise funds for the charity. In the principality she would visit old people's homes and hospitals, where she would put those white gloves to good use, running them across shelves and cubicles to check for cleanliness. From her very first year in Monaco she also held an annual party for its children, which of course her own offspring attended and greatly enjoyed.

---

*I*f there is one area from Grace's later years that should inspire us, it's this unerring dedication to charitable and noble causes. Of course, not all of us have the luxury of the money or time enjoyed by our heroine. Nevertheless, it's worth thinking about how much time we dedicate to the causes that we believe in. As such, and in honor of Grace's much-admired charitable and philanthropic nature, here's a brief guide to help you take positive action of your own.

○ Consider your values and core beliefs, then look for a charity or group campaigning on their behalf. Now take some time to help them out: you might stuff envelopes, help write newsletters, or take part in demos or Internet campaigns, or if you're really pushed for time, even sharing news and events on social networking sites such as Facebook or Twitter goes some way toward spreading the word.

○ Perhaps you have more time and energy. Why not try a sponsored run or walk (it might help keep you in shape, too!)? If you make this an annual event, you can have the satisfaction of knowing that once a year you are doing something practical for a good cause.

◗ Money talks. Can you spare a little each month for your favored cause? You may not think it much, but if everybody did the same, just think how much could be raised for those causes you strongly believe in. If you're one of life's planners, you could even leave your favorite charity a bequest in your will.

A PATRON OF THE ARTS

As the years rolled by, Grace became active in attracting new cultural activities to Monaco. In fact, she was in a creative frenzy in the late seventies. First, she revived Monaco's balletic tradition in creating The Monte Carlo Ballet. And as Rainier softened his attitude toward her beloved theater, in one of her proudest accomplishments Grace took over the Beaux-Arts Theatre. It opened shortly before her death and was subsequently renamed after her. Farther afield, in 1976 she began a series of poetry readings at the Edinburgh Festival, which received rave reviews. It was to be a busy year for Grace. That same year she was invited to be the first woman on the board of directors of 20th Century Fox, and the following year, 1977, she narrated the voiceover for *The Children of Theatre Street*, the fascinating tale of the Kirov School of Ballet in Russia. This may not have been the kind of role that Grace was used to, but it allowed her to keep a hand in all things showbiz.

Even though she had given up her beloved acting, in later life Grace supported others in similar creative endeavors: spiritually, practically, and financially. We love this philanthropic side, showing as it does her generosity of spirit and bigheartedness. If she could not be an active participant in the arts, then she would be a passive one, cheering on her fellow actors from the wings.

So, as we get close to calling a "wrap" on Grace's life story, if you wish to gain your certificate after being schooled in everything la Kelly, one last thing you must do is to promise us this: if you've been forced to give up on your own hopes and dreams, you'll consider helping others with their aspirations, as Grace did. And you never know, by keeping your hand in, you may be able to keep those pangs of nostalgia at bay. Manage this, and we're pleased to confirm you'll be a Class A Kelly student.

LEGACY

At the time of writing, it has been almost thirty years to the day since the death of Her Serene Highness Princess Grace of Monaco. However, the legend of Grace Kelly lives on. This might sound a little trite but this is one case where an overused phrase has its basis pretty much in fact. Books like this one are still being written about her, many a tree has died in our devotion to reading column inches on the subject, and of course her movies still leave movie fans agog, being some of the finest in cinematic history. But before we take a moment to consider why she remains such an enduringly iconic figure, let's take a whistle-stop tour of the many references to Grace in contemporary pop culture, and of the events and the celebrations of her life that continue to this day.

POP MUSIC

Mika, the British singer-songwriter born a year after her death, recorded a song named after Grace in 2007, while in 1990 Madonna paired Grace with Jean Harlow as a "beauty queen" in her monster hit "Vogue."

THE ARTS

In 2003, a play starring Rosamund Pike about a Hitchcock-obsessed film lecturer was staged in London's West End. *Hitchcock Blonde* owed its success in no small part to that enduring iconic image of Grace and her "sexual elegance" so much admired—and exploited—by Hitchcock on celluloid.

TV

In Season Four of the hit TV show *Gossip Girl* socialite Blair Waldorf marries Prince Grimaldi of Monaco in a story line with strong echoes of Grace's own life.

FILM

As we go to press, the first pictures of Nicole Kidman playing Grace in the forthcoming (2014) biopic *Grace of Monaco* have been released. Australian mega-actress Kidman appears stunning and elegant in the photos—almost as if she was born to play the role. The movie, set during the period in 1962 when Charles de Gaulle and Prince Rainier III were in dispute over Monaco's status as a tax haven, can't be said to portray the most glamorous era of Grace's life, but with director Olivier Dahan of the award-winning *La Vie en Rose* at the helm, we're sure Grace fans are in for a dramatic and emotional treat.

CELEBRATIONS AND EVENTS

In 2007, the nephew of François Mitterrand, Frédéric, staged an exhibition titled *The Grace Kelly Years* at the Grimaldi Forum in Monte Carlo. Then, in 2010 London's Victoria and Albert Museum took the material from this exhibition and ran a new one, celebrating Grace's innate sophistication and style. *Grace Kelly: Style Icon* was a sell-out and has since toured other world cities. Most recently, the Lighthouse gallery in Toronto ran an exhibition called *Grace Kelly: From Movie Star to Princess*, which ran for several months.

THE GRACE KELLY FOUNDATION

Following her death, Prince Rainier set up a charity to continue the amazing work done by Grace in helping young and emerging artists realize their career goals. "Now in its 30th year," states the home page of the charity's Web site, "the Foundation continues its mission to assist performing artists in honor of Princess Grace." Exciting news was reported from the charity in 2012: "In the year of the 30th anniversary of her death the charity foundation of the legendary screen actress is announcing a grants program for budding filmmakers." We can imagine how proud this would have made the philanthropic film-loving Ms. Kelly.

GRACE KELLY, THE MUSICAL

Of all the celebrations of Grace's life, this next one makes us want to sing with joy and try and reach that top note, as Grace did in *High Society*: *Grace*, composer Cy Coleman's musical about Grace Kelly that had its world premiere in Holland in 2001, is now being adapted for an English-speaking audience with American backers. The idea certainly strikes the right note with us.

Celebrations of Grace's life and career also took place during her lifetime. In 1982, the year of her death, the Annenberg Institute of Communications held a tribute to her film career in Philadelphia. That night the stars were out in force to congratulate Grace, who, overwhelmed with love for her peers and overjoyed to be remembered twenty years after she'd turned down the plum role in *Marnie*, said: "What can I say? I am overwhelmed and so filled with love, I would just like to hug every one of you." That same year a biopic about her life was to be screened, starring Cheryl Ladd. This time Grace was not amused. She even tried to have the movie banned, enlisting the aid of Frank Sinatra to do so, but even "Ol' Blue Eyes" could not dampen the public's enthusiasm for the first story of the life of the Hollywood Queen who became a princess. Luckily for Grace, though she would never see the movie, she was not too dismayed by the script. "They are trying to do it well and it will be fairly accurate," she wrote in a letter to Rita Gam just before her death.

What, then, was Grace Kelly's legacy? The movies, certainly; also Monaco became a popular tourist destination. On a personal note, we think it's safe to say that her most cherished legacy would be her children. Though there have been hiccups along the way, the family are now settled. Princess Caroline performs many of the duties previously carried out by her mother and is married to her third husband, Prince Ernst August of Hanover with whom she had her fourth child. Princess Stephanie has had trouble shaking off her wild child image. Having tried her hand at modeling, singing, and designing swimwear, she now concentrates on charity work (she is an ambassador of HIV and has set up her own HIV charity, Fight Aids

Monaco), and though she has three children, her personal life still provides plenty of fodder for the circling sharks of the press. As to the reigning Sovereign Prince of Monaco, Grace's only son, Albert, stories about his personal life, including fathering two children, could feed an entire banquet of story-hungry journalists—a situation that was not helped by the "ugly rumors" circulated out of jealousy, according to the Palace of Monaco, prior to his 2011 marriage to Princess Charlene.

As to their happiness, we shouldn't underestimate the loss of a mother at a young age. When Barbara Walters interviewed Princess Caroline in 1985, Caroline movingly said: "You're alone in the world, when your mother dies." And yet we are sure it would be a comfort to Grace to know that after her death Rainier continued to be a doting parent, and had been a hands-on grandparent too, looking after Stephanie's and Caroline's children as he did and being seen often with them in public before his death in 2005 following several weeks in the hospital suffering from heart, kidney, and lung problems. And when it came to Albert's two illegitimate children, we'd hope that Grace would love them just as much, with that big heart she was so well known for. . . .

LEAVING YOUR MARK

There's a poignancy to watching Pierre Salinger's TV interview with Grace, filmed just two months before she died, as he discusses with the princess how she would like to be remembered. We've noted throughout this book her thoughts on the matter: as a wife and mother, as a kind and decent human being, and aside from doing her job well, with little mention of her dazzling film career. Which makes us wonder about our own legacy . . . and *yours*. How would *you* like to be remembered? You may laugh; maybe you are only in your twenties, thirties, or forties, or even older still, and perhaps you have given the consequences of your life and death little thought. But just think what Grace had achieved by the time she was fifty-two: not one but two careers, an enormous contribution to charity and the arts, three children, and limitless fond memories for family and friends. Quite simply, it's common sense and very Grace-like to plan for your future and consider your own bequest to the world. So, in her memory, here are a few ideas for thinking about your own legacy:

PERCHANCE TO DREAM

Remember dreamtime from chapter one (page 19)? Now would be a good time to revisit the techniques used there to think about what you want from life and how you would like to be remembered. Pencil in a day to yourself, take a notepad, and wander the streets before finding a solitary spot. Close your eyes and imagine where you would like to be in ten, twenty, thirty years' time and how those around you will hold you in their memories. Can you conjure up an image of somebody—Grace aside—in whose footsteps you would like to follow? Would you like to be remembered as a Diana, charitable and kind, or as a Marilyn, a sensual bright star? Either way, make a note and envision yourself taking your idol's shape.

Writing the Last Words

This might seem morbid but why not pen your own obituary as you would like it to read. Which words float in front of your eyes? Do you envisage bountiful words written about your successes as a professional or a creative type, or a more personal account of your life as a wife, sister, mother, or girlfriend? No matter what your aspirations, try and envision a life lived without regret, having had the courage to spend time on this planet doing just what you wanted. Think about that. What kind of life would it be? It might seem a little crazy to be thinking of your deathbed, but it can be life affirming, too. Just try it!

Family Tree

Perhaps the only legacy you may wish to leave is your children. As we know, Grace wanted to be remembered in terms of her children, and family was hugely important to her. Of course family planning could have a whole book devoted to it, so we won't go into the whys and wherefores of having children here. But if you haven't had children already and that biological clock is tick-tick-tocking, it might be worth taking time out to assess whether you want kids as part of your legacy.

Make Your Mark

Do you want to make your mark on the world, or are you simply happy to sit on the sidelines watching as others shine in the limelight? It's better to decide sooner than later. And how will you make that mark if you are more of a doer than a cheerer-on? A creative endeavor is one way of ensuring you make an impression on the world at large. Can you act, sing, write, direct? Recording your ideas in words or pictures is one sure-fire way of ensuring your legacy will live on—and it doesn't hurt as much as childbirth, as we're sure Grace would agree!

THE FINAL CURTAIN

Although she had predicted her death in a car crash, we are quite sure Grace had not envisaged dying so young. In the year of her death (1982), TV interviews aside, Grace was not thinking of her own mortality. Instead she was plotting and planning for her future, with several projects on the go, and looking forward to the freedom that her last child leaving home would afford her and Rainier. "I always have lots of plans and projects," she said. Would she return to acting, even? "I've always tried to say never and always," she replied.

Friends report that in the early 1980s Grace was in better spirits than she had been for years. Her health had been suffering (Grace had been plagued by intolerable headaches), yes, but her metaphorical plate was still piled high with morsels of work and fun. "So much to do and so little time," she told her high school and lifelong friend Charlotte Winston by telephone in August 1982. That "much to do" included: a program of poetry recitals, a tour of four cities in order to find donors for a London theater project, and the completion of filming for a project on which she was working called *Rearranged*.

Rearranged was directed by Robert Dornhelm, with whom Grace had worked in 1977 (*The Children of Theatre Street*). It was to be her first cinematic role since *High Society*, playing herself in a comedy of mistaken identity set in Monaco's annual flower show. At half an hour long, it was not long enough to be a feature but nevertheless Grace had shown it to friends and family at a premiere and it had been well received. The idea was to finish filming and, with Rainier's blessing, send it to a TV network in the States. Upon her death, however, Rainier refused the filmmakers permission to have the work released.

The weekend of her death Grace had not been feeling well—"full of allergies and colds"—and had quarreled with daughter Stephanie about her relationship with car-racer Paul Belmondo. It was in this mood that she reluctantly agreed to drive Stephanie from Roc Angel in France to return to the palace, but on the journey home Grace suffered a small stroke that caused her to lose her footing on the pedal on a hairpin bend. She suffered a second, larger stroke as the car rolled off the hillside and would not survive, while Stephanie suffered such severe injuries that she could not attend her mother's funeral, five days later.

Attended by royalty, both heads of state, and the Hollywood variety, Grace's funeral took place on September 18, 1982. Her Mass card read: "Lord, I ask not why you have taken her away. I thank you for having given her to us." The obituaries came in thick and fast, mainly focusing on her movie career. "HOLLYWOOD LEGEND, THE END OF A FAIRY TALE, MONACO MOURNS" was just one of many headlines. The daily paper from her hometown, the *Philadelphia Daily News*, was factual about the details of her life and career; also kind in saying that her life had been a storybook: "For the fans, her name is Grace and her title Serene, and the storybook will never really close."

At her eulogy, James Stewart's heartfelt words sum up our heroine's many wonderful qualities.

You know, I just love Grace Kelly. Not because she was a princess, not because she was an actress, not because she was my friend, but because she was just about the nicest lady I ever met. Grace brought into my life as she brought into yours, a soft, warm light every time I saw her, and every time I saw her was a holiday of its own. No question, I'll miss her, we'll all miss her. God bless you, Princess Grace.

What first springs to mind when you think of Grace Kelly? Perhaps you are a fashionista and your thoughts turn first toward that look, those clothes, that style . . . Or maybe you're a movie buff and the words of Grace Kelly are synonymous with fireworks over the Riviera, negligee-clad women in rear windows, and drunken socialites—that is, her most iconic moments on film. Or perhaps you're a royalist and your first thought was Princess Grace, Her Serene Highness of dignity, hard work, and tradition.

For us, having come to Kelly first as film fans, we might once have fallen into the second category, but having researched this book our thoughts have become more complex. When we picture her now we think of a cornucopia of wonderful qualities: of fun and flirtation, of beauty and brains, of conscientiousness and sheer strength of character, too. We think of a magical woman whose storybook life has hopefully taught us a lesson or two, and who knows, if we follow those lessons in our own lives, maybe some of that old Grace magic will rub off on us, too?

ACKNOWLEDGMENTS

I've been very lucky to have had input on this book from editorial teams on two sides of the Atlantic. Firstly, I'm grateful to Aurum Press in the UK, whjo commissioned the book in the first instance, and to Barbara Phelan and Melissa Smith at Aurum for their insightful editorial comments. Across the pond, it's been thrilling to see the US edition go into production, so huge thanks to Lauren Marino, Susan Barnes, and all at Gotham Books for making this happen and for their support and advice.

For his patience and loyal support during the writing process, I'm thankful, as always, to my "prince" and husband, Roly Allen. My wonderful girlfriends have also been there for me at times of need. Mathilda Gregory in particular had some great ideas for the In the Movies chapter, and was always there to discuss Grace over a coffee or something stronger.

I was very lucky when *What Would Grace Do?* was first commissioned to have visited the wonderful *Grace Kelly: Style Icon* exhibition at London's Victoria and Albert Museum. Luckier still I visited the exhibition with two very glamorous women, my sisters Rhona and Rhiannon. My elder (and equally glam) sister Laura did not make the outing, but they are all three very stylish ladies and are truly an inspiration in all matters sartorial.

Grace Kelly's life story has been well documented down the years in a number of compelling biographies. These have been hugely helpful to me for research purposes, so thank you to Wendy Leigh, James Spada, Donald Spoto, and Robert Lacey in particular, for revealing so much about the life of this extraordinary woman.

Last but not least, thank you to Grace Kelly, and to her fans—long may her legend live on.

Bibliography

For those who wish to further their studies in the ways of Grace, herewith a list of helpful sources:

Britten, Fleur, *Debrett's Etiquette Guide for Girls*, Debrett's Limited, 2006

Brown, Bobbi, *Bobbi Brown Makeup Manual*, Headline Springboard, 2008

Cassini, Oleg, *In My Own Fashion: An Autobiography*, Simon & Schuster, 1987

Cohen, Juliet, *Vogue Beauty*, Carlton Books, 2001

Cousins, Mark, *The Story of Film*, Pavilion, 2004

De La Hoz, Cindy, *A Touch of Grace*, Running Press, 2010

Haugland, Kristina; Lister, Jenny; Safer, Samantha Erin, *Grace Kelly Style*, V&A Publishing, 2010

Lacey, Robert, *Grace*, Pan Books, 1995

Leigh, Wendy, *True Grace: The Life and Times of an American Princess*, JR Books, 2007

Life magazine, *Remembering Grace*, Time Life Inc., 2006

Maxford, Howard, *The A–Z of Hitchcock*, Batsford, 2003

McCann, Graham, *Cary Grant: A Class Apart*, Fourth Estate, 1996

Spada, James, *Grace: The Secret Lives of a Princess*, Doubleday, 1987

Spoto, Donald, *High Society: Grace Kelly and Hollywood*, Hutchinson, 2009

Spoto, Donald, *Spellbound by Beauty: Alfred Hitchcock and His Leading Ladies*, Hutchinson, 2008

Taraborrelli, J. Randy, *Once Upon a Time: The Story of Princess Grace, Prince Rainier and Their Family*, Pan Books, 2004

Tennyson, Alfred, Lord, *The Works of Alfred Lord Tennyson*, Wordsworth Editions, 1994

Truffaut, François, *Hitchcock: A Definitive Study*, Simon & Schuster, 1985

Wasson, Sam, *Fifth Avenue 5 A.M.: Audrey Hepburn, Breakfast at Tiffany's, and the Dawn of the Modern Woman*, Harper, 2010

Weil, Christa, *It's Vintage, Darling! How to be a Clothes Connoisseur*, Hodder & Stoughton, 2006

PRESS

Daily Mail, March 26, 2010

Globe and Mail, November 4, 2011

Guardian, October 26, 2011

Hartford Courant, December 29, 1954

Hartford Courant, Margaret Kelly, "My Daughter Grace," January 1956

Life, April 11, 1955

Luddington Daily News, January 5, 1956

Milwaukee Journal, September 15, 1982

Paris Match, "Grace and Rainier," March 17, 1956

Philadelphia Daily News, September 15, 1956

Scotsman, March 28, 2010

The New Yorker, Anthony Lane, "Hollywood Royalty," January 2010

Time, "The Girl in White Gloves," January 1955

Vogue, "Princess Grace of Monaco," March 1, 1972

Washington Post, April 18, 1956

Xperedon Charity News, March 15, 2012

FILMOGRAPHY

ABC 20/20 News Productions, Pierre Salinger, 1982

Barbara Walters Special: Interview with Princess Caroline, 1985

Grace Kelly Princesse de Monaco, Frédéric Mitterand, Grimaldo Forum Monaco, 2007

Grace Kelly: The American Princess, ILC Media Limited & Janson Media, 2007

Together Again, Mel Brooks and Dick Cavett, Brooksfilms Productions for HBO, 2010

GRACE KELLY FILMOGRAPHY

14 Hours, 20th Century Fox, Dir: Henry Hathaway, 1951

The Bridges at Toko-Ri, Paramount, Dir: Mark Robson, 1954

The Country Girl, Paramount, Dir: George Seaton, 1954

Dial M for Murder, Warner Bros., Dir: Alfred Hitchcock, 1954

Green Fire, MGM, Dir: Andrew Marton, 1954

High Noon, United Artists, Dir: Fred Zinnemann, 1952

High Society, MGM, Dir: Charles Walters, 1956

Mogambo, MGM, Dir: John Ford, 1953

Rear Window, Paramount, Dir: Alfred Hitchcock, 1954

The Swan, MGM, Dir: Charles Vidor, 1956

To Catch a Thief, Paramount, Dir: Alfred Hitchcock, 1955

WEB SITES

www.gracekellyonline.com

A Tribute to Grace and Excellence

www.montblanc-tribute-to-grace.com/en/index.html

NOTES ON SOURCES

A number of quotations in this book are unattributed in the text; those quotations and their sources are as follows:

p.10 last role Donald Spoto, *Spellbound by Beauty*, Hutchinson, 2008, p.149

p.25 she knew how Donald Spoto, *High Society*, Hutchinson, 2009, p.94

p.26 not to have Donald Spoto, *High Society*, Hutchinson, 2009, p.37

p.40 I really wasn't Donald Spoto, *High Society*, Hutchinson, 2009, p.77

p.44 Hitch wanted her Donald Spoto, *Spellbound by Beauty*, Hutchinson, 2008, p.147

p.49 It was a dog Donald Spoto, *High Society*, Hutchinson, 2009, p.122

p.51 She was the Graham McCann, *Cary Grant*, Fourth Estate, 1996, p.214

p.58 Every man who Howard Maxford, *The A–Z of Hitchcock*, Batsford, 2003, p.129

p.67 As far as Robert Lacey, *Grace*, Pan Books, 1995, p.137

p.68 He was mad Robert Lacey, *Grace*, Pan Books, 1995, p.183

p.69 There was something Robert Lacey, *Grace*, Pan Books, 1995, p.186

p.76 We were in love Oleg Cassini, *In My Own Fashion*, Simon & Schuster, 1987, p.268

p.77 a very charming Oleg Cassini, *In My Own Fashion*, Simon & Schuster, 1987, p.259

p.81 Grace's usual outfit Donald Spoto, *High Society*, Hutchinson, 2009, p.22

p.82 I have to Kristina Haugland with Samantha Erin Safer, edited by Jenny Lister, *Grace Kelly Style*, V&A Publishing, 2010, p.30

p.83 It makes your legs Donald Spoto, *High Society*, Hutchinson, 2009, p.19

p.85 Handbags are major Christa Weil, *It's Vintage, Darling!*, Hodder & Stoughton, 2006, p.193

p.92 Sex on screen François Truffaut, *Hitchcock*, Simon & Schuster, 1985, p.199

p.92 classical, beautiful Ibid., p.201

p.103 All women really Bobbi Brown, *Bobbi Brown*, Headline Springboard, 2008, p.4

p.105 Achieving the appearance Juliet Cohen, *Vogue Beauty*, Carlton Books, 2001, p.89

p.116 A little too Kristina Haugland with Samantha Erin Safer, edited by Jenny Lister, *Grace Kelly Style*, V&A Publishing, 2010, p.27

p.121 daffy Robert Lacey, *Grace*, Pan Books, 1995, p.185

p.121 I was Jewish Ibid., p.239

p.146 He has me J. Randy Taraborrelli, *Once Upon a Time*, Pan Books, 2004, p.217

p.148 enclosed J. Randy Taraborrelli, *Once Upon a Time*, Pan Books, 2004, p.259

p.151 Manners Fleur Britten, *Debrett's Etiquette for Girls*, Debrett's Limited, 2006, p.11

p.153 this ability J. Randy Taraborrelli, *Once Upon a Time*, Pan Books, 2004, p.216

p.153 **It was our** Robert Lacey, *Grace*, Pan Books, 1995, p.379

p.165 **Frankly,** J. Randy Taraborrelli, *Once Upon a Time*, Pan Books, 2004, p.97

p.172 **For a while** Donald Spoto, *High Society*, Hutchinson, 2009, p.108

p.174 **We just don't** Donald Spoto, *High Society*, Hutchinson, 2009, p.195

p.177 **How can I** Robert Lacey, *Grace*, Pan Books, 1995, p.372

p.180 **She was a** Donald Spoto, *High Society*, Hutchinson, 2009, p.73

p.180 **I don't know** J. Randy Taraborrelli, *Once Upon a Time*, Pan Books, 2004, p.351

p.181 **The princess's** J. Randy Taraborrelli, *Once Upon a Time*, Pan Books, 2004, p.220

p.182 **No matter where** Donald Spoto, *High Society*, Hutchinson, 2009, p.73

p.183 **Writing by hand** Fleur Britten, *Debrett's Etiquette for Girls*, Debrett's Limited, 2006, p.190

p.184 **No admonitions** Donald Spoto, *High Society*, Hutchinson, 2009, p.220

p.188 **To build up** François Truffaut, *Hitchcock*, Simon & Schuster, 1985, p.226

p.189 **a schoolboy** Donald Spoto, *High Society*, Hutchinson, 2009, p.135

p.191 **the hero's** François Truffaut, *Hitchcock*, Simon & Schuster, 1985, p.243

p.207 **Scorpio should never** J. Randy Taraborrelli, *Once Upon a Time*, Pan Books, 2004, p.87

p.207 **found a way** J. Randy Taraborrelli, *Once Upon a Time*, Pan Books, 2004, p.276

p.207 **Rainier was often** J. Randy Taraborrelli, *Once Upon a Time*, Pan Books, 2004, p.391

p.214 **They are trying** Donald Spoto, *High Society*, Hutchinson, 2009, p.214

p.218 **So much to** J. Randy Taraborrelli, *Once Upon a Time*, Pan Books, 2004, p.402

Index

A

Aga Khan (Prince Aly Khan)
     69, 134
Albert II, Prince of Monaco 96,
     172, 175, 215
Alexander technique 28
American Academy of
     Dramatic Arts 22, 23, 63,
     81
Andrews, Frank 208
Armstrong, Louis 53
arts, the 210–13
astrology 205, 206–7
Aumont, Jean-Pierre 69, 121,
     122, 123, 187

B

Bacall, Lauren 23, 124
Baker, Josephine 181
ballet 29, 210
barbecues 195–6
Barbizon Hotel, New York
     22–3
Beatrice, Princess 155, 156
Beaux-Arts Theatre, Monaco
     210
Belmondo, Paul 219
Bergman, Ingrid 187
Binns, Graham 185
biopics 212, 213–14
birthdays, remembering 182–3
blonde bombshells 110–15,
     190–1
Brando, Marlon 69, 153
Breen, Joseph 74
Brown, Bobbi 103
Burton, Richard 185, 205

C

Cambridge, Duchess of 11, 83, 94, 159
Caroline, Princess 85, 136, 146, 151, 153, 159, 172, 174, 175, 177, 180, 214, 215
Carroll, Madeleine 187
Cassini, Oleg 44, 62, 76–7, 81–2, 133, 147, 167, 184, 187
celebrations of Grace Kelly's life and career 211–14
Chanel, Coco 81, 84
charitable causes 143, 150, 160, 208–10
Charlene, Princess 215
Christensen, Helena 31
Churchill, Winston 181
classic clothes 82
cocktail parties 193–5
Coleman, Cy 213
Coleman, Herbert 58
comedy, romantic 53–4, 140
compromise, art of 46, 50

Conant, Howell 25, 102, 173
Cooper, Gary 37, 66
Crawford, Joan 25, 36
Crosby, Bing 47, 53, 68, 73, 114, 121, 139
Crystal, Billy 186
Curtis, Tony 69

D

dating 73–6
dental care 109
Designing Woman 124, 128
destiny 205–8
Diana, Princess of Wales 83, 155, 156–61
Dior, Christian 107
disappointments, shrugging off 39
Dornhelm, Robert 185, 218
dream diary 20
dreams and aspirations
    following 19–22, 55, 128
    legacy, planning your 216–17
    one thing at a time 128
    overcoming hurdles 23
    positive thinking 21
    self-belief 22
    self-help books 21
    wish lists 20–1
Dunne, Irene 125

E

elocution 30
Ericson, John 56
ESP 51, 207–8
evening gowns 88, 93

F

family values 163–77
father-daughter relationships
163–6
mother-daughter
relationships 167–71
parenting 174–7
fans, relating to 57–8
fashion and style see Grace
Kelly Look
father-daughter relationships
163–6
films
14 Hours 37, 59, 137–8
The Bridges at Toko-Ri 49,
68
The Country Girl 46–8, 50,
59, 68, 69, 96, 98, 112, 137,
139, 203
Dial M for Murder 42–3,
64, 67, 74, 83, 93, 98, 112,
114, 188
Green Fire 49, 50

High Noon 25, 37–9, 59, 66,
97, 138
High Society 25, 52–4, 73,
88, 99, 114, 124, 168, 171,
203
Mogambo 39–41, 66, 70–1,
97, 114, 180, 182
Rear Window 25, 36, 44–5,
58, 71–2, 88, 93, 98, 112,
137
Rearranged 218
The Swan 10, 36, 52, 59,
123, 140–1, 170
To Catch a Thief 50–2, 72,
84, 88, 92, 98–9, 168, 169,
190
flaws, overcoming 30
Ford, John 40, 42
friendships 179–96
birthdays, remembering
182–3
in all walks of life 182
keeping in touch 183–4
male/female friendships
186–7
muses 189
parties 193–6
with your ex 187
fun, having 52

G

Gable, Clark 36, 40, 66–7, 70, 71
Gam, Rita 63, 64, 125, 129, 175, 181
Gardner, Ava 56, 66–7, 70, 71, 92, 134, 180, 182
Garland, Judy 48, 56
Gaulle, Charles de 148, 212
Gillmore, Margalo 53, 168, 171
good causes, supporting 209–10
Grace Kelly Foundation 213
Grace Kelly Look 79–99
Granger, Stewart 49
Grant, Cary 26, 50, 51, 58, 72, 92, 134, 180, 191
grooming 107–9
Guinness, Alec 140

H

hair care 108, 114
handbags 85–7
Haya, Princess 145, 155, 156
Hays Code 74
Head, Edith 25, 44, 83, 84, 116
Hedren, Tippi 191
Hepburn, Audrey 79, 115
Hitchcock, Alfred 10, 41–2, 43, 44, 50, 51, 52, 54, 61–2, 64, 91, 92, 134, 187–91

Holden, William 47, 68, 139
Holm, Celeste 53, 152
Hopper, Hedda 67

I

instincts, following 44, 127–8, 136
Iran, Shah of 69, 121

J

jewelry 84, 87
Jolie, Angelina 38
Junot, Phillipe 177
Jurado, Katy 38, 39

K

Kanter, Jay 44, 140
Kelly bag 84, 85–7
Kelly, George (uncle) 31, 36, 63
Kelly, Grace (Princess Grace of Monaco)
  acting career 10, 22–3, 31–3, 35–59, 125, 214
    see also films
  beauty and physique 24–5, 101–17
  biographies 65
  charity work 143, 150, 160, 208–9
  death 161, 204, 208, 219

destiny, belief in 205–8
early life 17–19, 22–3, 150,
   164–5
engagement and marriage 9,
   94, 119–20, 123–4,
   129–30, 131–6, 157
family values 163–77
friendships 179–96
fun-loving 151, 180
funeral 219
health problems 18, 167,
   218
hospitality 192, 196
ice maiden aura 44, 46, 51,
   91–3, 152
legacy 211–12, 214–16
Little Black Book 197–201
manners 56, 150
miscarriages 172
modeling career 24–5, 27–8,
   29, 31
motherhood 10, 146, 158,
   172–7
myopia 59
patron of the arts 210–11
perfectionism 10, 208
photogenic quality 24–5, 29
political skills 148, 189, 212
princess role 143–61

relationship with Rainier
   139, 144, 146, 153–4, 184,
   203–4, 207
religious faith 205
romances 11, 44, 61–77,
   153, 184–5
style icon 11, 79–99, 159
tributes to 211–14
warmth 13, 151, 152
work ethic 19, 33, 37, 56,
   149–50, 150
Kelly, Jack (father) 11, 18, 19,
   22, 37, 62, 63, 64, 67, 103,
   123, 126, 127, 132, 163,
   164, 165, 166
Kelly, John ("Kell," brother) 18,
   77, 167
Kelly, Lizanne (sister) 18, 64,
   66, 68, 69, 126, 128, 132,
   167, 172
Kelly, Margaret (mother) 30,
   63, 65, 67, 69, 77, 81, 103,
   164, 167
Kelly, Peggy (sister) 18, 19, 63,
   132
Kennedy Onassis, Jackie 44, 79,
   134, 181
Kidman, Nicole 212

L

lace 93, 94
Lacey, Robert 65, 103
Ladd, Alan 68
Ladd, Cheryl 214
Leigh, Wendy 65, 66, 69, 93,
    175, 208
Lennon, John 31
less is more 49, 92–3
Letizia, Princess 145
letter writing 183–4
Levy-Soussan Azzoaglio,
    Louisette 57–8, 151, 185
life lessons
    beauty and grooming 105–9,
        114–15, 117
    compromise, art of 46, 50
    dating 73–6
    disappointments, shrugging
        off 39
    dreams and aspirations
        19–22, 55
    flaws, overcoming 30
    fun, having 52
    Grace Kelly Look 79–99
    Grace-inspired formulas 33,
        58
    instincts, following 44,
        127–8, 136
    less is more 49, 92–3
    manners 56, 150–1, 152
    obligations, fulfilling 50
    opportunities, making the
        most of 31
    poise and posture 24–5,
        26–9, 82
    remaining true to yourself
        45, 152
    something new, trying 54
    speaking up for yourself 43
    work ethic 19, 33, 37, 56,
        149–50
    see also dreams and
        aspirations; family values;
        friendships; marriage;
        parenting; weddings
lipsticks 114
love letters 184
Lund, John 73
Lyons, Gene 64

M

McMullen, Jim 182, 185
Madonna 211–12
makeup 105–7, 114
manicures 108
Mann, Delbert 32
manners 56, 150–1, 152
Marnie 54, 189–90, 191
marriage

husband, choosing a 126–7,
141
rocky patches 137–8, 154
standing by your man 138,
139
media, handling 57, 111, 159,
161
meditation 20
Meisner, Sandy 38
MGM 36, 40, 47, 49, 50, 54,
57, 124, 125, 129
Mika 211
Milland, Ray 64, 67
Mitterrand, Frédéric 91, 213
Monroe, Marilyn 51, 56, 92,
110–13, 115
Monte Carlo Ballet 210
mother-daughter relationships
167–71
muses 189
music tributes 211–12, 213–14

N

Niven, David 134, 153, 184–5,
205
North by Northwest 191
Novak, Kim 191

O

Oberon, Merle 125
Oliver (poodle) 180
Onassis, Aristotle 134
opportunities, making the most
of 31

P

paparazzi 57, 111
parapsychology 207–8
parenting 174–7
discipline 175–6
making time for your
children 174–5
teenagers, rearing 177
traditional 176–7
Parker, Dorothy 196
parties
barbecues 195–6
cocktail parties 193–5
Parton, Dolly 115
pedicures 108
perfumes 109
Perlberg, William 47

Pike, Rosamund 212
pilates 28
poise and posture 24–5, 26–9,
82
Positive Mental Attitude
(PMA) 21
pout 115

Q

Quine, Judith 181, 184

R

Rainier III, Prince of Monaco
53, 54, 104, 119–20,
122–3, 125, 126, 129–30,
131–2, 139, 141, 144, 146,
153–4, 165, 173, 174, 177,
181, 184, 189, 203–4,
207–8, 213, 215, 218
Ratoff, Gregory 116
Richardson, Don 63, 75, 187
Robyns, Gwen 182, 185
Rose, Helen 48, 59, 82, 94, 99,
129
roses 133, 134
Royce Landis, Jessie 168, 169,
170
Russell, Jane 92

S

Saint, Eva Marie 191
Salinger, Pierre 125, 152, 176,
215
Saltzer, Robert 93
scarves 87
Schary, Dore 40, 41, 49, 127,
140
Schiller, Friedrich 135
Seaton, George 46, 48
self-belief 22
shoes 109
Sinatra, Frank 53, 54, 69, 73,
134, 153, 154, 180, 214
Sinden, Donald 66
skin care 105
smoking 105
Snowdon, Lord 104
Spada, James 66, 68
sponsored runs/walks 209
Spoto, Donald 55, 65, 66, 68,
174, 205
Stephanie, Princess 172, 175,
177, 214–15, 219
Stewart, James 45, 58, 71, 124,
143, 219
studio system 36
sunglasses 87, 90–1

T

tarot 207
Taylor, Elizabeth 185, 205
teenagers, rearing 177
Truffaut, François 92, 188, 191
Turlington, Christy 105
twin sets 88

V

Vertigo 191
vintage style 85–6, 89, 194

W

Walk of Fame, Hollywood 59
Walters, Barbara 136, 173, 175, 215
Wang, Vera 94
wardrobe
    accessories 84–5
    capsule wardrobe 87–9
    care of 108
    less is more 92–3

wedding gown, Grace Kelly's 59, 94, 129, 131
Wedding in Monaco 129
weddings
    attention to detail 134
    entourage 133
    fairy-tale weddings 135–6
    Grace Kelly's wedding 119–20
    guests 135
    hiccups 131
    venue 131
    wedding dress 132
white kid gloves 81, 95, 209
Wii Fit 28
Winston, Charlotte 181, 218
wish lists 20–1
work ethic 19, 33, 37, 56, 149–50, 150

Y

yoga 28